Jackson and Bunny hopped through the empty silent streets until, as dawn was breaking, they reached the docks.

'Look!' cried Jackson as they made their way along the cobbled quay. 'There's a ship!'

Tied up alongside was a great three-masted sailing ship, whose sides towered above the two little rabbits.

'How ever shall we get aboard?' said Bunny.

'The same way that the sailors do,' said Jackson. 'Follow me!' And he ran along the quay until he reached the foot of a long narrow, wooden gangplank . . .

All Because of Jackson won the Bronze Medal for the 6-8 age category of the 1996 Smarties Prize.

DICK KING-SMITH
All Because of Jackson

Illustrated by
John Eastwood

YOUNG CORGI BOOKS

ALL BECAUSE OF JACKSON
A YOUNG CORGI BOOK : 0 552 528218

First published in Great Britain by Doubleday,
a division of Transworld Publishers

PRINTING HISTORY
Doubleday edition published 1995
Young Corgi edition published 1997

9 10

Set in Bembo Schoolbook by
Phoenix Typesetting, Ilkley, West Yorkshire

Young Corgi Books are published by Transworld Publishers,
61–63 Uxbridge Road, London W5 5SA,
a division of The Random House Group Ltd,
in Australia by Random House Australia (Pty) Ltd,
20 Alfred Street, Milsons Point, Sydney, NSW 2061, Australia,
in New Zealand by Random House New Zealand Ltd,
18 Poland Road, Glenfield, Auckland 10, New Zealand
and in South Africa by Random House (Pty) Ltd,
Endulini, 5a Jubilee Road, Parktown 2193, South Africa.

Printed and bound in Great Britain by
Cox & Wyman Ltd, Reading, Berkshire.

CONTENTS

CHAPTER ONE

Jackson was a seaside rabbit.

He was born in a sandy burrow on top of a cliff, and as soon as he was old enough to come out and sit on the grass and look down at the sea, he was fascinated by it.

While his brothers and sisters played about in the clifftop field, Jackson would sit by himself and watch the waves rolling in to break upon the sandy shore.

He watched the tides go in
and out, he watched the seabirds
wheeling and diving, and
especially he watched the tall
sailing-ships gliding past in the
distance. How beautiful they are,
thought Jackson. How I should
love to run away to sea and be
a sailor.

He consulted his mother.

'Mama,' he said.

'Yes, Jackson?'

'There are men on those ships,
aren't there?'

'Yes, Jackson. Sailors.'

'I should like to be a sailor,
Mama.'

'Silly boy,' said Jackson's mother. 'Rabbits don't go on ships.'

'But Mama, the sea is in my blood.'

'You go on a ship,' said his mother, 'and your blood will be in the sea. Men eat rabbits.'

Jackson went away to think about this. I could hide, he thought. There must be lots of places to hide in a big sailing-ship. I could be a stowaway. I won't tell Mama or Papa. I'll just go.

So he did.

He set off across the clifftop field very early one morning, determined to find where the sailing-ships came in. That evening, climbing wearily to the top of a far headland, he looked down and saw before him just what he wanted.

There below was a wide bay,

and on its shores a large seaside
town with a great harbour, in
which lay a number of tall ships.

Tired out, Jackson found an
empty rabbit burrow and
crawled into it.

'Tomorrow,' he murmured as
he drifted into sleep, 'tomorrow I
shall go aboard my ship.'

CHAPTER TWO

That night Jackson had the weirdest dream.

He was, it seemed, in a strange country, not cool and rainy like his homeland, but dry and very hot. Suddenly he saw the most extraordinary animal.

It was as tall as a man, with reddish fur, ears like a donkey, and a face like a sheep. Its arms were short, and it stood upright, balanced upon two enormously strong legs and a long, thick tail. Then the dream turned into a nightmare, for the monstrous creature began to come towards him, not walking, not running, but hopping in huge bounds on those great hind legs. And as it drew near, Jackson could see something even more frightening. On the animal's stomach was a sort of pocket, and out of this pocket poked another head, with ears like a baby donkey and a face like a lamb!

Jackson woke with a squeal of terror.

'What's eating you?' said a voice, and there beside him in the burrow was another rabbit, a young doe of about his own age.

'I was having a bad dream,' he said.

'In my burrow,' said the other.

'Oh, sorry!' said Jackson. 'I didn't know. By the way, my name's Jackson.'

'Funny sort of name.'

'Not really. My father's called Jack. Anyway, who are you?'

'My mother doesn't believe in naming children,' said the young doe. 'She's had so many, she can't be bothered. She just calls us all "Bunny".'

'Bunny?' said Jackson. 'That's nice. I like it.' And I like you, he thought. I wonder if . . .

'You don't fancy going to sea, do you, Bunny?' he said.

'To sea?'

'In a ship. To sail away over the ocean.'

'Where to?' said Bunny.

'I don't know,' replied
Jackson. 'That'll be half the fun
of it, not knowing.'

'But rabbits don't go on ships,'
said Bunny.

'This one's going to,' said
Jackson. 'I want to sail the seas.
I want to see the world.'

'You're crazy,' Bunny said.
But nice, she thought.

'Well,' she said, 'it'll be
daylight before very long. We'd
better get started.'

When they reached the town, Jackson and Bunny hopped through the empty silent streets until, as dawn was breaking, they reached the docks.

'Look!' cried Jackson as they made their way along the cobbled quay. 'There's a ship!'

Tied up alongside was a great three-masted sailing-ship, whose sides towered above the two little rabbits.

'How ever shall we get aboard?' said Bunny.

'The same way that the sailors do,' said Jackson. 'Follow me!' And he ran along the quay until he reached the foot of a long, narrow, wooden gangplank. It was nearly broad daylight by now and there were noises on board, bangings and knockings and men's voices and footsteps.

'Quick!' said Jackson. 'Up we go!' And up they went, scampering up the gangplank on whose side was fixed a large printed notice.

Brave British Hearts!
To all those of an
Adventurous Spirit
wishing to seek their fortunes and start a new life in a far country, take note that the Peninsular & Oriental Navigation Company's Clipper
Atalanta
will set sail for
AUSTRALIA
on the
Third day of April 1842

CHAPTER THREE

The moment that Jackson and
Bunny reached the top of the
gangplank, they saw to their
horror a number of sailors busy
swabbing down the decks.
Luckily the men's backs were
towards the two rabbits, who
instantly dashed for cover.

A frightened rabbit goes
straight underground, and
though here there was no
ground to go under, Jackson
saw nearby a large,
square, black
hole,

and into it he dived head first,
Bunny following. Down the
hatch they fell.

As well as passengers, the
Atalanta was carrying in her hold
goods for the settlers in Australia,
and, luckily for the rabbits (for
they fell a long way), it was a
cargo of bales of cloth. On these
Jackson and Bunny landed and
bounced.

'Are you all right, Bunny?' gasped Jackson.

'Yes, I think so. Where are we?'

'In a very big burrow by the look of things,' said Jackson. 'A good place for us to stow away, I should think.'

'Would you?' said Bunny.

'Well, yes. We can hide amongst all this stuff. No-one will ever find us. We can spend the whole voyage down here.'

'And at the end of the voyage,' said Bunny, 'how exactly do we get out again?'   Jackson looked up at the open hatch, high above. He scratched one ear thoughtfully with a hind foot.

'Ah,' he said.

'And while we're down here,' went on Bunny, 'what exactly do we eat?'

'Ah,' said Jackson again.

'Or drink?'

'Ah,' said Jackson. 'Yes. Hm.' But before he could add to this, they heard the sound of footsteps on the deck above, and voices, and then suddenly the square of daylight vanished as the hatch cover was put back, leaving the hold of the ship in darkness.

'It had better be a very short voyage,' said Bunny. 'Otherwise it would seem to me that, without food or water, we shall not see much of the world after all. We shall simply die down here. And all because of you, Jackson.'

All that morning the two rabbits hopped about in the gloom, exploring the great stack of bales of cloth that covered the floor of the hold, and finding nothing else.

Above them, there was much hustle and bustle on deck as the passengers came aboard, and then, around midday, a sudden great crash of sound as a brass band struck up on the quayside.

In amongst its noise the rabbits could hear voices bellowing orders, and the cries of farewell of those who were leaving and of those who had come to wave them goodbye.

Then, when the music had stopped and the shouts and calls had died away, peace and quiet returned as the *Atalanta* nosed her way out of harbour, and set sail for her journey to the opposite side of the world.

Down in the hold, Jackson
and Bunny felt the motion as the
clipper met the open sea, and
heard the creaking of her
timbers. Squatting side by side
on a bale of cloth, the rabbits
rose and fell as the ship swooped
and dipped over the waves.

'Jackson,' said Bunny.

'Yes?'

'I don't feel very well.'

'Me neither.'

'I don't think I'm a very good sailor.'

'Nor me.'

'I wish I hadn't come.'

'Me too,' said Jackson. 'I'm sorry I got you into all this, Bunny. It's all my fault. I shall regret it for the rest of my life.'

Bunny snuggled up to him. 'Don't worry,' she said. 'That won't be long.'

By the following day the rabbits had grown used to the motion of the ship. They had also grown extremely hungry and thirsty.

When the ship had been some days at sea, the captain ordered an inspection of the various holds, to see that each was watertight and that their cargo had not shifted.

By now too weak and miserable to care, the rabbits watched helplessly as the hatch cover was removed, and a seaman climbed down a ladder, carrying a lantern.

A big, bearded man, he shone the light about as he examined the bales of cloth, and then its beam fell full upon the wretched stowaways.

'Well, I never!' said the seaman softly. 'You'll make a nice meal, my hearties, you will!'

Afterwards, Jackson and Bunny couldn't really remember what happened, so weak and helpless were they.

In fact, the bearded seaman found a sack and popped them in it, and climbed the ladder out of the hold, only to meet the first mate at the hatchway.

'All shipshape down below, Jenkins?' said the mate.

'Aye, aye, sir,' replied Jenkins.

'What have you got in that sack?'

The seaman heaved a sigh.

He'll have 'em off me, he
thought, that's for sure.

'Rabbits, sir,' he said.

'Rabbits?' said the mate.

'Yes, sir,' said Jenkins. 'Found
'em in among the bales. Don't
know how they come to be there.'

The mate opened the mouth
of the sack and peered in.

'Well, well!' he said. 'They'll
make a nice meal. Take them
down to the galley and tell the
cook I'll have them for my supper.'

'Aye, aye, sir,' said Jenkins
dolefully, but before he could
move, the captain of the *Atalanta*
appeared, an imposing figure
with mutton-chop whiskers,
a gold-peaked cap upon
his head, and a
brass telescope
under his arm.
'What's all this,
Mister Mate?' he said. 'What has
that man got in that sack?'

The first mate heaved a sigh.
He'll have 'em off me, he
thought, that's certain.

'Rabbits, sir,' he said.

'Rabbits?' said the captain.

'Yes, sir,' said the mate. 'Open the sack, Jenkins.'

'Well, well,' said the captain. 'I'm very partial to a nice young rabbit, or better still, two nice young rabbits, under a good, light, pastry crust, with some strips of fat bacon.'

He put a hand into the sack and felt the limp forms within.

'Found 'em down below, did you, Jenkins?' he said.

34

'Yes, sir.'

'Heaven only knows how they got there,' said the captain, 'but one thing's sure. They'll have had no food or water since we sailed. They're as weak as kittens. We must put some flesh on them first. Jenkins, take them to my cabin steward and tell him to see to their needs.'

'Aye, aye, sir,' said the seaman.

'And Mister Mate,' said the captain, 'I'd be obliged if you'd

have a word with the ship's carpenter. Tell him to knock me up a cage for my rabbits, and to bring it up to my cabin when it's done.'

'Aye, aye, sir,' said the mate.

'One thing's sure,' said the captain. 'Once my rabbits have grown a bit and fattened up, they'll be well worth waiting for. I shall enjoy them, Mister Mate. They'll make a nice meal.'

By great good fortune, the captain's cabin steward was a rabbit fancier. Ashore, he kept a shed full of tame ones, and under his expert care Jackson and Bunny soon recovered their health and strength.

Amongst the stores of food that the *Atalanta* had loaded for her voyage was a plentiful supply of vegetables, still fresh, and the two young rabbits gorged happily on cabbage-leaves and carrot-tops and turnip-greens.

In addition, the steward fed them broken bits of ship's biscuit, and generally looked after them very well. In due course, he knew, the captain would eat them, but that was what rabbits were for.

'Tuck in, my dears,' he said, stroking their brown backs. 'Enjoy life while you can.'

And indeed they did.

'It's funny, you know,' said Jackson to Bunny. 'Mama told me that men eat rabbits, but that doesn't seem to be true.'

'They're certainly treating us well,' said Bunny with her mouth full. 'Both the little one who feeds us and the big one with the whiskers who stands and stares at us. I'm really quite enjoying this voyage now.'

'Me too,' said Jackson. 'I wonder where we shall end up?'

In the captain's pie-dish was of course the answer to this question, and some weeks later the cabin steward's expert advice was sought.

'You keep rabbits at home, Tompkins, don't ye?' said the captain.

'Yes, sir.'

'What d'ye think of these two now? Fit to eat, would you say?'

'Well, sir,' said the steward, 'they're not yet fully grown. I don't reckon they were more than two month old when they come aboard. And we've been at sea eight weeks – that makes 'em four month old now.'

'Another four weeks' sailing,' said the captain, 'and we'll reach Australia. I want to make a meal of them before then.'

'Was you going to eat the both of them yourself, sir?' asked the steward.

I was, thought the captain, when they were littler, but now . . . maybe I should give a little dinner, for Sir Hereward and his lady, with rabbit-pie as the main course.

Sir Hereward Potts was a rich and important merchant in the city of London, sailing to Australia with the intention of

becoming the richest and most important merchant in the city of Sydney. He was much the most notable of the *Atalanta's* passengers. A favourable report to the Peninsular and Oriental Navigation Company from Sir Hereward Potts would do the captain no harm at all, and the rabbit-pie would do Sir Hereward a power of good.

'Eat both of them myself, Tompkins?' said the captain in reply to the steward's question. 'Of course not. I shall invite Sir Hereward and Lady Potts to share such a treat.'

That evening the captain of the *Atalanta* asked the merchant and his wife to his cabin for a glass of wine, and proposed the little dinner party.

'Tomorrow, at about this hour?' he said. That should give Tompkins ample time to see to the preparation of the pie, he thought.

'Delighted, Captain,' said Sir Hereward.

'Too kind,' said Lady Potts.

Then she caught sight of Jackson and Bunny, lolloping happily about in their cage.

'Oh!' she cried. 'How I do love rabbits!'

'So do I,' said the captain. 'They are to be the main attraction of our little dinner tomorrow. They are still young and should be very tender, I have no doubt.'

Much to the captain's surprise, Lady Potts gave a little scream of horror.

'Oh, Captain!' she cried. 'Oh, you could not! Surely you do not mean to kill those charming little creatures? Oh, I could not bear to think of such a thing, much less eat them. Oh, Hereward, must they be slain?'

'My wife is tender-hearted, Captain,' said Sir Hereward, and he did not look best pleased.

The captain thought fast.

'I do apologize for suggesting such a thing, your Ladyship,' he said. 'I had not realized . . . so thoughtless of me.'

Stupid woman, he thought,
now I shan't be able to eat
them, she'll be for ever asking
me how they are. There's only
one thing to do.

'Sir Hereward,' he said with a
little bow, 'I wonder – would
you permit me to present these
animals to Lady Potts as a gift,
in token of my esteem?'

Sir Hereward looked doubtful.

'The rabbit is unknown in Australia,' went on the captain, 'and the possession of these two specimens would be in keeping with your wife's position as a leader in colonial society.'

Lady Potts gave another little scream, this time of delight, and cried, 'Yes! Oh, Captain, yes, how kind of you. Pray have them removed to our quarters for the remainder of the voyage. We shall be delighted to have them, shall we not, Hereward?'

And though Sir Hereward Potts' word was law to thousands in the world of business, he knew better than to cross swords with his wife.

'Yes, my dear,' he said. 'Delighted.'

Thus it was that for the remaining four weeks of the voyage of the *Atalanta* to the Antipodes, the stowaways found themselves in the lap of luxury. Jackson and Bunny were petted and fondled and fed upon the choicest of titbits, and allowed the freedom of the Potts' stateroom for much of the day, while, with dustpan and brush, a steward cleaned up behind them.

When at last, at the end of her three-month voyage, the clipper *Atalanta* entered Sydney Harbour, the rabbits were in beautiful condition: fat, sleek and strong.

Sir Hereward had taken a house in the country, some way outside Sydney, and to this he travelled by coach with his wife and all their many pieces of baggage. Among these was the rabbit cage, covered with a sheet to conceal the inmates from prying eyes, for Lady Potts intended to surprise the colonials with her unusual pets.

When they arrived she insisted that the rabbit cage be unloaded first and placed upon the lawn.

'I must let my little friends stretch
their legs,' she said to her husband,
and she removed the sheet and
opened the door of the cage.

Jackson and Bunny hopped
out and looked about them.

'We seem to have arrived,'
said Jackson.

'But where?' said Bunny.

'I have no idea.'

'Will they not run away, my
dear?' said Sir Hereward.

'Run away?' said Lady Potts. 'What an idea! They are much too tame and much too fond of me, are you not, my dears?' And she bent to stroke them.

'Bunny,' said Jackson. 'Are you thinking what I'm thinking?'

'Yes,' said Bunny. 'Let's go!' And side by side they raced away, the first rabbits ever to set foot upon Australian soil.

CHAPTER EIGHT

After all those months cooped up in the *Atalanta* it was sheer bliss to be out in the fresh air again, out in the sunshine (and very hot sunshine it was), and to be free once more.

Jackson and Bunny ran and ran, just for the joy of running, and leaped and twirled and buckjumped (or in Bunny's case doejumped) in the highest spirits, delighted with one another.

When at last they stopped and looked about them, it was to see a countryside very different from their cool damp homeland. The grass was more brown than green, and the blue-gums looked

nothing like English trees. The birds that they saw were strange too – screeching cockatoos and laughing kookaburras and flocks of parrakeets and budgerigars.

Then suddenly Jackson saw a large shape in the distance.

'Quick! Hide!' he said to Bunny, and they scurried for the shelter of some tussocky grass.

'What's the matter?' said Bunny. 'You're trembling.'

'My dream!' said Jackson. 'Do you remember, when we first met in your burrow, I'd been having a bad dream?'

'Yes, I remember.'

'Well,' said Jackson, 'here it comes!' And peering through the grass stems, Bunny saw the most extraordinary animal.

It was as tall as a man, with reddish fur, ears like a donkey, and a face like a sheep. Its arms were short, and it stood upright, balanced upon two enormously strong legs and a long thick tail. Then this monstrous creature began to come towards them, not walking, not running, but hopping in huge bounds on those great hind legs. And as it drew near, Bunny could see something

even more frightening. On the
animal's stomach was a sort of
pocket, and out of this pocket
poked another head, with ears
like a baby donkey
and a face like
a lamb!

'Don't move,' whispered Jackson. 'It may not see us.' And the two rabbits froze, crouching low with ears laid flat back and eyes bulging with terror.

With one last hop the great red kangaroo landed right beside their hiding-place and looked down at them out of her mild sheep's eyes. From her pouch her joey looked down too.

'Ma,' he said. 'What kind of animals are those?'

'No idea, son,' said the mother kangaroo. 'Never seen such strange-looking creatures in my whole life. Hold tight now.'

And away she bounded.

'Fancy calling *us* strange!' said Bunny. 'I never set eyes on such weird things as those before.'

As time passed, Jackson and Bunny were to see a great many other odd-looking beasts. As well as kangaroos, they met wallabies and bandicoots and opossums and koalas and numbats and wombats and many more.

There were familiar creatures as well, like cattle and a great many sheep, but one sort of animal they never met.

'It's funny, isn't it?' said
Jackson one day. 'In this place
where we've landed up,
wherever it is, there are no other
rabbits.'

'No,' said Bunny, 'but there
soon will be.'

'I don't understand,' said
Jackson.

But a little later he did, for
Bunny scratched herself a nest-
burrow and there gave birth to
five babies.

'Aren't they lovely!' said Jackson, and indeed, he must have liked babies, because by the end of the rabbits' first year in their new country, Bunny had produced four more litters, totalling twenty-two young in all, and by then she and Jackson were already great-grandparents!

Contents

Introduction

This book has been written for students learning about Information and Communication Technology in secondary schools. It provides a comprehensive background to go with the practical skills which are learnt at Key Stages 3 and 4. The book contains the material required by the National Curriculum and the syllabus content for the Edexcel, OCR and AQA examination boards for GCSE ICT courses and ICT short courses.

The world of computing and communications is changing at such a rate that no textbook will remain up-to-date for more than a couple of years. This book, now in its fifth edition, is based on the latest developments relevant for the 2002 syllabuses.

Information and Communication Technology is an exciting subject and understanding the theory as well as the practical skills will benefit all students.

Using this book

If this is your own book, you may decide to personalise it. Use the margin to make notes and the space provided with the questions to pencil in your answers before checking them with the answers given at the back of the book. The contents pages have been designed in the form of a checklist so that you can monitor and assess your progress as you work through the book.

The index at the back of the book will help you to find specific topics. Answers to the questions are provided on pages 116 and 117.

Feedback

If you have any comments or suggestions as to how this book may be improved, please send them to the author via Pearson Publishing.

1 Types of computer

For many years, computers have been placed into different groups according to their size, performance and cost. With the rapid development in computer technology, a new group has appeared, the personal digital assistants (PDAs), and the traditional minicomputer group is largely disappearing as microcomputers and computer networks become more powerful. The different groups are described below:

- supercomputers
- mainframe computers
- minicomputers
- microcomputers
- PDAs
- embedded computers.

Supercomputers

Supercomputers are the fastest and the most expensive computers. They have huge processing power and are used mainly for scientific and engineering applications. This power makes them suitable for applications such as weather forecasting and complex graphical techniques. A supercomputer currently being built by IBM (International Business Machines) will be able to perform 10 trillion mathematical calculations per second using 8200 processors working in parallel. Computers of this size and power can cost £100m.

Mainframe computers

Mainframes are used in large companies for data processing and by scientists for complex mathematical calculations. They can have hundreds of simultaneous uses. Mainframes have also found a new role as network servers on the Internet. On average, a mainframe would cost £4m. An example of a mainframe is IBM's System/390.

Minicomputers

Minicomputers may be used by smaller businesses to manage their data processing needs. Complex programs like relational databases run efficiently on these computers and older database programs can be linked to newer programs running on the Internet.

An example of a minicomputer is IBM's AS/400. The role of minicomputers is being replaced by microcomputers and computer networks as these become more powerful.

Microcomputers

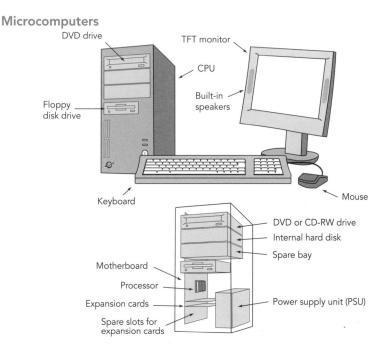

A modern desktop computer with cut-away showing internal features

Desktop computers

The computers we use at home, in school and in most businesses are called microcomputers. There are many different makes and models to choose from when buying a microcomputer but ones with a CD-ROM or DVD drive, stereo sound, a modem and software are available for around £1000. The type and speed of the processor broadly determine the power of the computer. A typical processor is the Intel Pentium 4 running at 1.4 Ghz (1400 million cycles per second). Since microcomputers were first introduced, the speed of processors has increased year by year. Several manufacturers are now shipping 64 bit processors running at 2 Ghz (1 gigahertz = 1000 megahertz). Although this trend is likely to continue, there has recently been a new demand on manufacturers to develop processors for portable devices like Internet mobile phones. These processors need to be smaller and use much less power in order to conserve the batteries in these portable devices.

Notebooks

Modern notebook computers are light and easy to carry around. They are approximately 30 cm across, 20 cm back and 3 cm deep and can weigh less than 1 kg. The screen is on the inside of the top flap that hinges open. Notebooks have many of the features that are available on desktop computers including CD/DVD drives, floppy disk drives, modems and the sockets at the back to connect to printers and monitors. The keyboards have the same layout as desktop computers although the keys are more compact and notebooks use touch pads or a button to control the screen pointer. For ultra-light and thin notebooks, the DVD and floppy drives can be placed in a docking station that also contains the battery charging unit and connections for the printer. The user will then slip the notebook into the docking station when they return home or go into the office. Although notebook computers have the advantage over desktop microcomputers in size, weight and portability, they are usually not as powerful, are more expensive and will not allow standard expansion cards to be slotted in.

Personal digital assistants (PDAs)

These are small hand-held computers generally only 12 cm long by 8 cm wide and less than 2 cm deep. These personal electronic organisers have software for keeping a diary, holding contact details, making notes, sending and receiving emails and playing games.

Because they are so small, most PDAs use a touch-sensitive screen and a stylus (pen) rather than a keyboard to input data. Software is then used to recognise either the user's handwriting or accept letters selected by the stylus from a screen display of the keyboard. Docking stations are often used with PDAs so that batteries can be recharged and data, for example, diary entries, can be updated with desktop PCs.

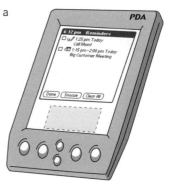

Embedded computers

From telephones to missiles, and from cameras to washing machines, many modern devices contain built-in computers or embedded systems. There is no need for these systems to use keyboards and computer monitors since the inputs required come from the device's sensors, and outputs control the operation of the device.

2 Structure of a computer

The diagram below shows a simple structure for the operation of a computer. Data is obtained for processing by the computer and then the results of the processing are output from the system:

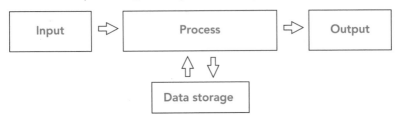

Input

The need to capture data quickly and accurately has led to a wide range of input devices. These input devices make use of human touch, light, magnetism, sound, control and electronic sensors. Each type of input device has been designed for a specific purpose.

Process

In home, business and school microcomputers, a main processing chip called the processor or central processing unit (CPU) handles the instructions from the computer program and processes the data. Computers with more than one processor chip are less common, but might be found at the centre of a school network acting as a file server.

Output

The results of processing are passed to output devices. The most common output devices are the computer monitor and the printer. Output devices are considered in *Chapter 4*.

Keyboard

The most common way of entering data into a computer is through the keyboard. The standard keyboard illustrated below is called a QWERTY keyboard as these letters are the first six keys on the top row of letters. The basic layout of the keys is similar across many countries in the world although slight variations exist where languages use additional letters in their alphabets.

Modern keyboards often have a support at the front of the keyboard as a rest for the typist's wrists and some manufacturers have designed keyboards with a more curved key layout in an attempt to make typing faster and more comfortable. In comparison with other input devices, entering data using a keyboard is quite slow, even for touch-typists who have learnt to type using all their fingers and thumbs without needing to look at the keyboard.

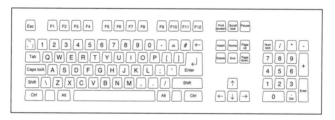

A QWERTY keyboard

Concept keyboard

A concept keyboard consists of a flat-bed of contact switches covered by a flexible membrane. Programmers can allocate one or more switches to respond in different ways. Overlays with pictures and symbols are placed over the membrane.

Uses of the concept keyboard include in primary schools where the overlays are designed with interesting picture layouts. Children press particular symbols or pictures in response to the activity being done. These keyboards are very flexible: an overlay for a five-year-old can be designed quite differently to an overlay for a ten-year-old which would be more detailed.

Concept keyboards are also used in restaurants where the checkout tills use symbols to speed up the data entry. They can also be used in hostile environments, for example, on North Sea oil platforms where the keyboard allows workers to use computer-controlled machinery through the keyboard without it being damaged by salt spray or chemicals on the platform.

Mouse

The movement of the mouse by the user's hand is mirrored by the pointer on the monitor screen. Under the mouse is a ball which rolls as the mouse is moved. This movement of the ball causes two shafts to rotate inside the mouse; one shaft records the movement in the north–south direction and the other shaft records the east–west movement. When the screen pointer is over an icon or menu selection, the mouse button can be clicked, double-clicked or dragged (moved with the button held down) to activate a process. Some mice have a small wheel as well as the buttons. The function of the wheel depends on the software being used on the computer: in a document, it can allow the user to scroll up and down; in a desktop publishing package, it might enable the user to zoom in and out of the page. Over a period of time, the performance of the mouse can deteriorate as the ball and shafts collect dust and dirt. Some modern mice use a light beam and detector to register movements instead of the mouse ball. Many mice now use infra-red or wireless links to the computer which removes the need to have a connecting cable.

Trackerball

A trackerball is similar to a mouse but the ball is set into a cup on the top of the unit. A finger or, on larger trackerballs the palm of the hand, is used to roll the ball in any direction. The ball controls the movement of the pointer on the screen. Buttons on the trackerball work in the same way as mouse buttons to activate processes on the screen.

Joystick

Joysticks are popular input devices for computer games. The hand grip can be moved around the central axis in any direction but is spring-loaded to return to the centre when the hand pressure is released. Joysticks have many more buttons to control the software functions, for example, when using a joystick to control a flight simulator, the buttons control the flaps, views from the cockpit, landing gear and engine speed. Some joysticks have 'force feedback' which enables the user to feel some of the forces that might be experienced in real life.

Graphics tablet

The graphics tablet is a flat pad which the user can write or draw on with a device similar to a pen called a stylus. The surface of the pad is sensitive to the position of the stylus and the stylus itself is sensitive to the pressure applied by the user.

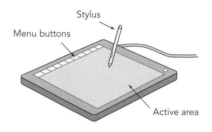

Stylus
Menu buttons
Active area

As the stylus is moved across the pad, the movement is translated to a drawing on the computer monitor. The harder the user presses on the stylus, the thicker the line drawn on the screen. A typical resolution for a graphics tablet used in art work and computer aided design (CAD) is $^{1}/_{1000}$ cm.

Interactive electronic whiteboard

This is similar in appearance to a normal whiteboard used in the classroom but behind the surface of the board is a grid of copper wires. When a normal marker pen is used on the board, the grid detects the position of the pen and relays the co-ordinates back to the computer. The image can be stored and shared across a network. Electronic whiteboards are most effective when used together with computer projection systems. Here the teacher can interact with the image being projected onto the whiteboard. For example, by using a special electronic pen which acts like a mouse, the teacher can select menus, manipulate images and run multimedia sequences to help deliver the lesson.

Touch screen

On touch-sensitive screens there are criss-crossing beams of infra-red light just in front of the glass on the computer monitor. When a user touches the glass with their finger, two sets of rays are blocked: the rays travelling from side to side and the rays going from top to bottom. The computer can detect the position of the finger from the light sensors placed on the opposite side of the monitor screen to the light sources, and respond accordingly (see diagram below).

Touch screens are easy to use (user-friendly) and might be found as input devices in public places (eg museums) with information software.

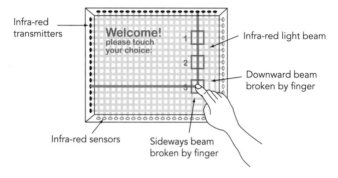

Touch screen

Scanners

Scanners enable both pictures and text to be input to a computer. Scanning text in order to recognise the words and letters requires special software (this is covered below under OCR). The most common type of scanner is the flat-bed but smaller and cheaper hand-held scanners which are rolled over the document/picture are also available.

The flat-bed scanner works by placing the picture to be scanned face down on a glass plate like a photocopier. A bright light is slowly moved across the picture and the reflected light is focused onto a light-sensitive device using several mirrors and a lens. White parts of the picture reflect the most light, black parts reflect the least and colours reflect different wavelengths of light. For each tiny part of the picture, the intensity and nature of the light is captured and converted into a digital signal for input to the computer. Scanned pictures, which can be manipulated using sophisticated image editing software, are often used in publishing work.

Optical character recognition (OCR)

Scanning devices using OCR software are used to recognise letters, numbers and words. The ability to scan the characters accurately depends on how clear the writing is. The software has improved to be able to read different styles and sizes of type and also neat handwriting.

One application of optical character recognition is reading postcodes on letters at sorting offices so that letters can be sorted automatically.

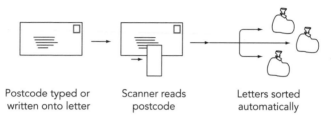

Postcode typed or written onto letter	Scanner reads postcode	Letters sorted automatically

Optical mark reader (OMR)

Optical mark readers detect marks made on paper. It is usually recommended that the marks are made with a soft (HB) pencil. The reader scans across the paper with an infra-red light. Where there is no mark, there is a strong reflection of light off the white paper; where a mark has been made, the reflection is reduced.

This form of input is often used for students' answers to multiple-choice examination papers and for selecting the numbers on lottery tickets.

Magnetic ink character recognition (MICR)

This method of inputting data into a computer is used on bank cheques. The important data on a bank cheque that is required when it is processed is printed along the bottom edge of the cheque as strange-looking characters. The ink used to form these characters contains tiny magnetic particles. This enables the data from each cheque to be read into the computer by machine. MICR is a fast and reliable method of reading data into a computer as it is unaffected by scribbling over the characters with a pen (see illustration page 100).

Bar code reader

Bar codes are made up of black and white stripes of different thicknesses. These lines represent numbers and are read with a wand or laser scanner. They are now used on almost all goods sold in shops and supermarkets, and provide a fast and reliable method of entering data even when the surfaces being read are curved or upside down.

The numbers of the bar code hold coded information about the product, including the country of manufacture, the name of the manufacturer, a product item code and a check digit. They do not hold information directly for the name, description or price of the product. When the numbers on the bar code are scanned, the data is passed to the computer which then returns information about the product.

Digital camera

The picture taken with a digital camera is stored in computer memory rather than on film as in an ordinary camera.

The different colours that make up the picture are converted to digital signals (codes of 0s and 1s) by sensors placed behind the lens. These pictures can then be displayed directly onto the computer monitor or imported into a graphics/art package for editing. The quality of the picture is determined by the resolution

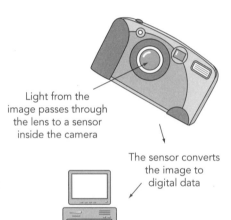

Light from the image passes through the lens to a sensor inside the camera

The sensor converts the image to digital data

The image can now be stored or loaded into a computer

of the camera and is measured in pixels (see page 15). High-quality digital cameras may have a resolution of three or more megapixels.

Many cameras have their own small LCD (see page 16) screen which displays the picture taken with the camera. This gives the user the option to view the picture and discard it if it is not suitable. The cost of taking pictures with a digital camera is much less than an ordinary camera where a film and processing has to be purchased. An ink-jet printer (see page 17) and high-quality paper is all that is needed for printing digital pictures.

Video capture

Digital camcorders can plug straight into computers via a Firewire interface. (A Firewire interface is the name given to a very fast data link between the computer and the digital camcorder.) This allows the computer to download, store and manipulate the digital video image.

Conventional camcorders can also transfer video into a computer, but because the image is held in analogue form, a video digitiser or video capture card is required to convert the signal into a digital format for storage and/or display on the computer (see page 69 for information on analogue and digital formats).

Video capture and editing requires computers with large hard disk drives since files containing video data tend to be quite large.

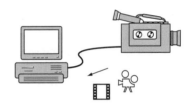

Captured files can then be edited in a number of ways, mixed together and compressed, to take up significantly less memory (as little as $1/100$ of the original size) with relatively low loss in image quality.

Musical instrument digital interface (MIDI)

MIDI was developed as a standard for linking musical keyboards together. Computers fitted with MIDI interface boards can be connected to MIDI instruments, allowing the music being played to be stored and displayed by the computer on the monitor. The computer can display the music as a musical score and notes can be added, altered or deleted. The music being played can also be printed out from the computer.

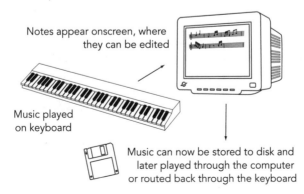

Notes appear onscreen, where they can be edited

Music played on keyboard

Music can now be stored to disk and later played through the computer or routed back through the keyboard

Magnetic stripes

Magnetic stripes are thin strips of magnetic tape, often found on the back of plastic credit and debit cards. When the card is used, the stripe passes playback heads, similar to a tape recorder, which reads data from the stripe.

Cards with stripes are used, for example, to withdraw cash from cash dispenser machines (called automatic teller machines or ATMs) in the walls of banks, building societies and shopping centres.

Smart cards

A smart card (also known as an integrated chip card, or ICC) is a plastic card that contains a tiny microprocessor chip. This enables more data to be stored on the card and also enables the personal identification number (PIN) entered by the user to be checked against the information held in the chip. Smart cards are more secure than cards with magnetic stripes but they have not been widely adopted by banks because of the cost of changing all the cash machines (ATMs). Smart cards are used more extensively in other European countries and in this country for mobile phones and satellite television receivers.

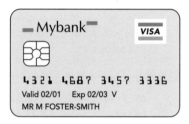

Speech or voice input

Speech or voice input is a rapidly developing means of input to a computer. It is already an important method for people who are severely handicapped, or where the user's hands need to be free to do other things, but it requires fast processing and large amounts of memory.

Programs are available which will recognise continuous speech input, translating the words directly into a word processor. Some words sound the same but are used in different contexts, eg 'weather' and 'whether' or 'sail' and 'sale'. These programs can select the appropriate spelling from the sentence that is spoken.

Switches

When computer input comes from mechanical devices like automated machinery in factories, switches can be used. Mechanical switches such as slide, toggle and push buttons are activated by the operator or moving equipment.

Proximity switches are activated when a magnet comes close to the switch. The two contacts which form the switch come into contact in the magnetic field. Tilt switches operate as the device is raised and lowered. Tilt switches can be gas-filled sealed units or mercury switches where a bead of mercury runs along inside the tube forming a contact.

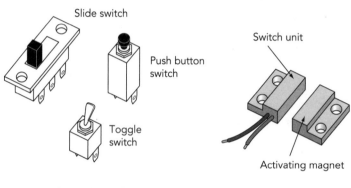

Slide switch

Push button switch

Toggle switch

Switch unit

Activating magnet

Some mechanical switches

A proximity switch

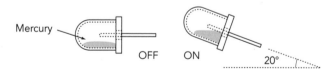

Mercury

OFF   ON

20°

A tilt switch

Thermistors

 Thermistors are devices that can be used to measure temperature since their resistance changes with temperature. Using this device, the computer can input the temperature and respond accordingly, perhaps by switching on or off other circuits controlling heaters.

Light-dependent resistors (LDRs)

 Light-dependent resistors are light sensors that change their electrical resistance according to the amount of light falling on them. The brighter the light, the lower the resistance. These, together with heat sensors, could be used in a computer automated greenhouse to maintain the ideal growing conditions for the plants.

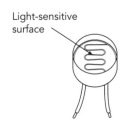

Light-sensitive surface

Light-dependent resistor

Questions

1 Name two input devices that might be used with a desktop publishing package in addition to the mouse and keyboard.

   ....

   ....

2 The bar code on a tin of beans contains which of the following pieces of information?

   ☐ Sell-by date   ☐ Country of manufacture

   ☐ Shop name   ☐ The size of the tin

3 Why are price details not part of the bar code?

   ....

   ....

4 Name an input device that could be used:

   a   to control conditions in an automated greenhouse ....

   b   by young children in a primary school ....

   c   to read the postcode on a letter ....

   d   to mark a student's multiple-choice answer paper ....

   e   to obtain money from a cash dispenser machine ....

4 Output devices

Monitors

 The computer monitor, screen or VDU (visual display unit) is the most common output device. Screen sizes are still quoted in inches and popular sizes are 15 inches (38 cm) and 17 inches (43 cm). The size is always measured diagonally, from corner to corner, but beware, the size of the screen you see is less than the quoted size as some of the glass is hidden behind the plastic rim of the monitor casing. The screen sizes for televisions are also measured in the same way. Larger monitors make working at a computer easier on the eyes and are essential for use in desktop publishing and design work.

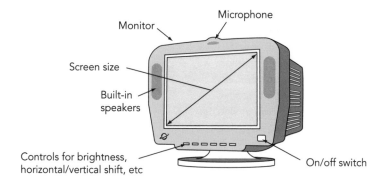

A monitor

Computer monitors are similar in many ways to the television. They use cathode ray tubes (CRTs) containing an electron gun at the back of the tube which fires electrons at phosphor dots coating the inside of the screen. When struck by the electrons, the phosphor dots glow to give the colours. Because you sit very close to a computer screen and need to be able to read small text, these dots need to be very close together. On a colour monitor, a set of dots is made up of a group of three colours: one green, one blue and one red dot. One group of dots is called a pixel (short for picture element) and a typical distance between the pixels on a computer monitor is 0.28 mm.

The spacing of the pixels determines the clarity, or resolution, of the screen image. Three standards in current use are:

- VGA (video graphics array)   640 x 480 pixels
- SVGA (super video graphics array)   800 x 600 pixels
- XGA (extended graphics array)   1024 x 768 pixels.

Most monitors utilise cathode ray tubes (CRTs) to display the image. However, notebook computers and the more modern flat-panel displays utilise liquid crystal displays (LCDs), thin film transistors (TFTs) or field emission displays (FEDs).

Liquid crystal displays (LCDs)

Liquid crystal displays utilise tiny crystals which, when a charge is applied across them, polarise the light passing through them. Used in combination with special filters, this means that light will not pass through when an electrical charge is applied. LCDs are also used in watches and calculators.

A slim and lightweight notebook computer with TFT screen

Thin film transistor screen

A more advanced type of display, giving a full colour and high quality output, is the TFT active matrix screen. Each pixel on the screen is controlled by its own transistor. This provides a higher resolution and more contrast.

Field emission displays

Field emission display screens use two thin sheets of glass a millimetre apart, separated by a vacuum. The back glass is made up of millions of tiny tips that can be switched on and off and fire electrons at the front screen across the vacuum. When the phosphor dots are hit by the electrons, they glow to produce bright, sharp images.

Printers

Over the years, many types of printers have been made with different print mechanisms. These printers can be placed in one of two groups – impact printers and non-impact printers. With impact printers, the letters, or tiny pins which make up characters, strike an inked ribbon against the paper. Because of this hammering effect, these printers can be quite noisy. Today, the most popular types of printer for schools, offices and homes are ink-jet and laser printers, which are non-impact printers.

Dot-matrix printer

A dot-matrix printer has a printhead that travels across the paper. In the head are a set of pins which shoot out and strike the ink ribbon against the paper as the printhead moves along. These printers produce low to medium quality black and white printing. Several years ago they were the ideal choice for a home printer but now the colour ink-jet has taken their place. They are still used in business for the following reasons:

- The running costs are very low.
- They are robust and can operate in harsh environments.
- If several sheets of self-carbonating paper are placed into the printer, then multiple copies can be produced at the same time. This is because it is an impact printer and strikes the paper. This is particularly useful in places such as warehouses.

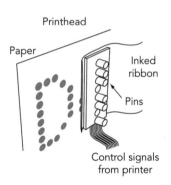

Ink-jet printer

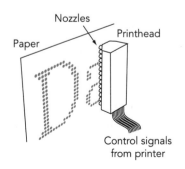

In an ink-jet printer, the printhead contains tiny nozzles through which ink can be selectively sprayed onto the paper to form the characters or the graphic images. Inside the printhead are tiny piezoelectric crystals. These crystals change shape when an electric current is applied across them and this forces the ink out through the printhead nozzle.

The bubble-jet printer is a type of ink-jet printer but instead of the ink being forced out of the printhead, it is heated rapidly. This causes the ink to boil and a bubble of ink is formed. As the bubble forms, it expands and is forced through the nozzle of the printhead and onto the paper. Ink-jet and bubble-jet printers are relatively inexpensive and produce high quality black and white or colour printing. This makes them a popular choice for home and school use. The printing speed is, however, slower than a laser printer so for most businesses where a greater printed output is required, the laser printer is more suitable.

Laser printer

Laser printers work on the same principle as photocopiers. The toner, which is powdered ink, is transferred to the paper where it is fused by the action of heat and pressure. Lasers are very quiet printers and give high quality print. A mono (black and white) laser printer with a speed of eight pages per minute (ppm) can be purchased for around £200. A school or business printer would have a typical speed of 12 to 24 pages per minute. The majority of laser printers sold are still mono but colour printers are becoming more popular as their prices are dropping to around £1000.

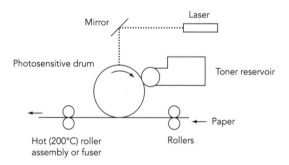

A laser printer

A laser printer works by the laser drawing the image onto a negatively-charged photosensitive drum. Where the laser hits the drum, the charge is removed. The drum then passes the toner reservoir where negatively-charged toner is attracted to these areas. This toner is then transferred to the paper, where it is heated, and made to stick by the fuser assembly.

Plotters

 There are several types of plotter. The flat-bed plotter, commonly found in the Design and Technology departments of schools, uses precision motors controlled by the computer. These motors move an arm across the paper in the 'x' direction and the pen unit up and down the arm in the 'y' direction. An electromagnet lifts and drops the pen onto the paper.

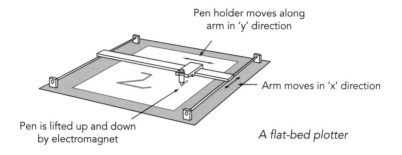

Pen holder moves along arm in 'y' direction

Arm moves in 'x' direction

Pen is lifted up and down by electromagnet

A flat-bed plotter

Plotters are often used in science and engineering applications for drawing building plans, printed circuit boards, machines and machine parts. They are accurate to hundredths of a millimetre and can be the size of a small classroom. However, the increase in the quality of low-priced A2 and A3 size colour ink-jet printers has reduced the demand for the new smaller plotters.

Sound/voice

 As well as having music played by the computer from programs or from CD-ROMs, it is possible to have spoken output. This is particularly useful for blind users where passages of text or figures from a spreadsheet are spoken by the computer. Speech synthesis is used by BT for their directory enquiries service. When you call directory enquiries and the operator has located the number for you, this information is given to you through a computer-synthesised voice. The telephone numbers are stored in a database and the computer reads out the number selected by the operator in the form "The number you require is...".

Light-emitting diodes (LEDs)

1.8-20 mm

 LEDs are small electronic components which emit light when a voltage is placed across them. LEDs are also used to monitor the logic state (ON and OFF) in control applications.

A light-emitting diode

Switching

Earlier, we looked at how switches could be used as an input device. Computers can also output signals to switch equipment and machines on and off. This control of equipment requires much greater electrical power than can be provided by the computer. It is therefore necessary to boost the computer's signal with special power-switching electronic components, eg silicon controlled rectifiers (SCR).

Actuators

 Signals from computers can generate physical movement in certain control devices. These devices are called actuators and include:

- motors
- hydraulics
- pneumatics.

Motors

The output of a computer can be used to drive small stepper motors. With stepper motors, each electrical pulse from the computer rotates the motor shaft by a tiny amount. For a typical motor this might be a turn of 1.8° which would mean 200 pulses would be needed to turn the shaft of the motor through one complete revolution.

A stepper motor

Stepper motors give very precise movements and can be used on devices such as flat-bed plotters or a robotic arm.

Hydraulics

Here the output from the computer controls the movement of hydraulic rams by pumping oil. These hydraulic rams, similar to those seen on mechanical diggers and bulldozers, can be slow but are very powerful.

Pneumatics

Pneumatics are quite similar to hydraulics in using rams but the pistons are powered by air rather than oil. Pneumatics are not as powerful as the hydraulic systems but the movement of the system is very fast.

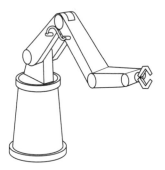

A robot arm can be controlled by motors, hydraulics or pneumatics. The type of system used depends on the application, ie:

- most accurate movement – motors
- the fastest movement – pneumatics
- most powerful – hydraulics.

Questions

1 Digital watches (see page 75) use microcomputers. Describe one input and one output device used.

....

....

2 Tick the devices used for output from a computer:

☐ Joystick ☐ Plotter

☐ Monitor ☐ Bar code reader

3 Choose the best printer for the following situations:

a A quiet, high quality, black and white printer for desktop publishing work ....

b A colour printer for use at home ....

c An impact printer that can print several copies at once using self-carbonating paper ....

4 For each output device listed below give an example of where it might be used:

a Speech from a voice chip ....

b Stepper motor...

c LCD display...

5 Computer memory

Bits

Computers are constructed of electronic circuits. Through these circuits there can be two states – electricity can be flowing or not flowing. When a pulse of electricity is present we call this a '1' and the absence of electricity is a '0'. The transistors on silicon chips can store a 'bit' (**B**inary Dig**it**) which is either the 0 or the 1.

Bytes

A byte is a unit of memory in the computer. It is made up of eight bits. In other words, a byte can store eight 0s or 1s. Each character from the keyboard is given a code consisting of eight bits. These codes are the same internationally and are called the ASCII code (American Standard Code for Information Interchange). The code for the letter 'a' is 97 or 01100001. Each character, therefore, is held in one byte of memory. One byte is a very small amount of storage and it is more usual to refer to kilobytes (KB), megabytes (MB) and gigabytes (GB).

- 1 kilobyte = 1024 bytes (2^{10})
- 1 megabyte = 1024 kilobytes = 1 048 576 bytes (2^{20})
  – approximately 1 million bytes
- 1 gigabyte = 1024 megabytes = 1073 741 824 bytes (2^{30})
  – approximately 1 thousand million bytes
- 1 terabyte = 1024 gigabytes = 1099511627776 bytes (2^{40})
  – approximately 1 million million bytes.

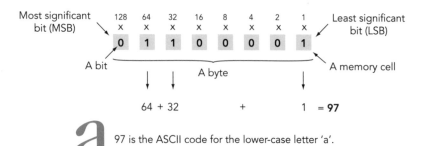

How the letter 'a' is stored in computer memory

All computers have memory to store instructions and data. There are two main types of memory:

- RAM (random access memory)
- ROM (read only memory).

Random access memory (RAM)

The typical amount of RAM in a microcomputer might be 128 megabytes. When the computer is switched off, this memory is empty. As the computer is started, operating instructions, computer programs and data are moved into this memory as required.

The diagram on the right illustrates a memory map for the RAM. The RAM clears when the computer is switched off, which is why it is important to save your work to disk when you finish.

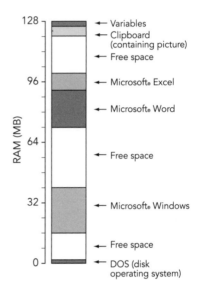

Read only memory (ROM)

ROM is memory stored in a chip which is not lost when the power is turned off. On most computers (eg PCs), this memory is quite small but it contains the essential instructions to enable the computer to check the hardware and load operating systems from the disk in order to start. RAM is referred to as volatile memory as the contents of the memory 'evaporate' when the power is switched off. ROM is non-volatile memory.

Question

Complete the sentences below by using the correct words from the following list: *memory   megabytes   eight   RAM*

"A home computer has 128 .... of .... memory.

A byte is a unit of computer .... It consists of

.... bits."

6 Data storage

A storage device retains its contents when the computer is switched off and is used to hold programs and data. All computers have some form of permanent storage.

Hard disks

Hard disks are a common form of data storage on most computers, both on stand-alone and networked computers. A typical microcomputer purchased for home or school would have a disk capacity of 10 or 20 gigabytes. This would hold the operating system (eg Microsoft® Windows), applications (word processor, spreadsheet, database, etc), games and the data from programs. On larger systems, the hard disks may hold terabytes (1024 GB) of storage.

Data is stored by magnetising the surface of a flat, circular plate. These plates rotate at high speed, typically 60 to 120 revolutions per second. A read/write head floats on a cushion of air a fraction of a millimetre above the surface of the disk. It is so close that even a smoke particle on the disk would cause the heads to crash. For this reason, the drive is inside a sealed unit.

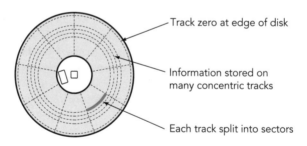

Track zero at edge of disk

Information stored on many concentric tracks

Each track split into sectors

Tracks and sectors on a disk

Programs and data are held on the disk in blocks formed by tracks and sectors. Moving directly to data on a disk drive is called random access.

Floppy disks

Floppy disk drives can be found on most microcomputers and accept the familiar 3.5 inch floppy disks. High density disks for a PC hold 1.4 MB of data. Floppy disks are useful for transferring data between computers and for keeping a back-up of work files. Back-up disks should be kept safely away from the main computer for security reasons.

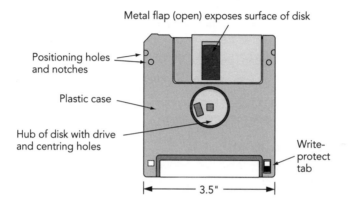

Metal flap (open) exposes surface of disk

Positioning holes and notches

Plastic case

Hub of disk with drive and centring holes

Write-protect tab

3.5"

Floppy disks only spin when loading or when saving data needs to take place. Floppy disks rotate more slowly than hard disks, at only six revolutions per second.

Disk access times

For a drive to read data from a disk, the read/write head must move in or out to align with the correct track (this is called the seek time). Then it must wait until the correct sector approaches the head. The time it takes to do this is called the disk access time. It sounds very short (about 15 milliseconds for a typical hard drive), but can be very significant when accessing or searching through large amounts of data (eg in a large database). Floppy disks and CD-ROMs have longer access times than hard disks.

Compact discs

Computer compact discs hold large quantities of data (650 MB) in the form of text, sound, still pictures and video clips (see page 67). The data is stored on the surface of the disc as minute indentations and is read by a laser light.

CDs are available in three forms:

- **CD-ROMs** – The letters ROM in the name mean read only memory. In other words, you can only read from the disc, not write or store data onto it. This type is the most common sort of CD available and is the way most software programs are sold. It is a memory storage device but would not be considered as a 'backing store' as the user cannot write to the disc.
- **CD–R** – These CDs are initially blank but, using a special read/write CD drive unit, the user can store programs and data onto the disc. These discs can only be written to once.
- **CD–RW** – These are similar to the 'R' type above but the user can read, write and delete files from the disc many times, just like a hard disk.

Both CD-ROMs and CD-Rs can be referred to as WORM devices. This stands for **w**rite **o**nce **r**ead **m**any times.

Digital video discs (DVDs)

Digital video disc (DVD) (sometimes known as digital versatile disc) drives are now replacing CD drives in computers. DVD RAM drives (writable drives) are still quite expensive but when they become more readily available, they may eventually replace home CD systems and VHS tapes as well. The success of DVD is largely due to the huge memory capacity of the disk and the high quality of stored images. DVDs can store up to 17 GB of data, the equivalent of 26 CD-ROMS (or the capacity of nearly 12 000 floppy disks). This equates to eight hours of full-motion images together with sound tracks and subtitles.

26 CD-ROMs at 650 MB each   1 DVD at 17 GB

Watching a film stored on DVD format has significant advantages over VHS video tape. The digital images and sound tracks produced from the DVD are of a higher quality and the user can move to any part of the film immediately. In addition, the high quality digital images and sound do not deteriorate with constant use as they do with the magnetic VHS tapes.

Magnetic tape

Magnetic tape can also be used for permanent storage. Data is saved along the tape in blocks, separated by 'interblock gaps'. Just like the tape in a tape-recorder, the data is written to or read from the tape as it passes the magnetic heads. One disadvantage of tape storage is that you cannot go directly to an item of data on the tape as you can with a disk. It is necessary to start at the beginning of the tape and search for the data as the tape goes past the heads – this is called serial access.

As magnetic tape is relatively cheap, tapes are often used to take a copy of hard disks for back-up (security) reasons. One popular magnetic tape unit, a similar size to a computer hard disk unit, is called a tape streamer. These units use tape cassettes that can store very large quantities of data, typically 26 GB. The cassettes can then be kept in a safe place away from the computer.

Removable media

There are other common devices, such as zip and jaz drives, which are similar to floppy drives, in that individual disks are removable and portable, yet they hold much larger amounts of data (typically between 100 MB and 2 GB).

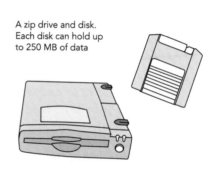

A zip drive and disk. Each disk can hold up to 250 MB of data

Questions

1 Games programs can be purchased from computer stores on CD-ROM. State two advantages of CD-ROMs over floppy disks.

    ....

    ....

    ....

    ....

2 Hard disks and floppy disks are both used to store data from a computer. Give two instances where floppy disks are used.

    ....

    ....

7 Operating systems

All computers use an operating system (OS). This is a complex program which controls the entire operation of the computer. It handles basic input and output such as data from the keyboard and output to the screen and also the transfer of data to disk drives. Although the illustrations (on pages 29 and 30) show different features of operating systems, practical systems combine these features. For example, a sophisticated OS could handle multiprocessors, users and tasks simultaneously. Examples of three well-known operating systems are:

- UNIX – was written in the computing language C and is a multi-user, multi-tasking OS, often found on larger systems like minicomputers and mainframes but increasingly on microcomputers.

- Microsoft® Windows 98/Me – a popular operating system used in PCs in homes, schools and businesses.

- Microsoft® Windows NT/Windows 2000 – a more complex multi-tasking operating system used in network environments. If you are using Windows 95 or 98 on a school network, then it is quite likely that the operating system being used by the network server(s) is running a form of Windows NT.

Tasks of an operating system

We have already said that an operating system is a complex program. Some of the tasks it needs to perform to ensure the efficient operation of the computer system include:

- allocating a slice of time with the processor for each job that needs to be processed

- ensuring that jobs with different priorities are dealt with in the correct order

- creating a balance between tasks which require a lot of processing time and tasks needing more use of peripherals like printers

- handling input and output and ensuring that input goes to the right program and output goes to the right place

- maximising use of the computer's memory by allocating different sections to the programs and data in use.

Methods of operation

There are a number of different ways in which computers are designed to operate. These include:

Single program mode – Just one program running on the computer at a time.

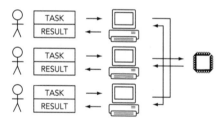

Multi-tasking (multi-program) mode – Here two or more programs can be run at once. The operating system ensures that the resources of the computer are shared, including the processor where each program shares the processor time.

Multi-user mode – Here several users can use the same system together and the operating system gives each user a share of processor time called a time slice.

Multi-processor mode – In larger systems, the computer will contain more than one processor. The operating system allows the different processors to operate together and share the same memory.

Batch mode – It is sometimes more efficient to collect together a group of programs or data, and then run this through the computer in one go or as a batch. An example of batch processing is running a payroll program. The wage data (eg hours worked) is batched together before the program is run to calculate the monthly wages. During batch processing, there is no user input.

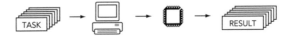

Real-time – Here the computer reacts immediately to incoming data and responds straight away. These inputs might come from sensors in an aeroplane running on automatic pilot by computer. A change to the plane's flight caused by air currents must be corrected immediately. Another example of real-time processing would include making a reservation for the cinema or for a coach trip. When reserving the seat, the computer will block others from taking the same seats even if they enquire a second later.

Computers running in real-time must be fast enough and have enough processing power to handle extreme situations.

Questions

1 Using the word list below, fill in the gaps in the following sentences:

real-time   memory   multi-user/multi-tasking   printer
multi-processor   batch   mainframe

"A computer that has more than one processor requires a

.... operating system. A network file server with one

processor requires a .... operating system.

When customers of a travel agent book their coach seats using the

Internet, this form of processing is called ....

When the travel agents calculate the monthly wages for their staff, they

are more likely to use .... processing."

2 Which of the following situations does not use real-time processing?

a an embedded computer-controlled washing machine

b asking directory enquiries for a telephone number

c a flight simulator package

d printing a telephone directory.

8 Human–computer interface

The way in which a computer user communicates with the computer is called the human–computer interface (or man–machine interface).

A good interface between the user and the computer program should be:

- friendly – being able to use the software without needing to read the whole manual first

- attractive – encourages users to use the software

- effective – it does the job it is designed to do efficiently

- easy to use – menu structures are consistent across packages (eg to save a program, users expect to find the option under the File drop-down menu).

Graphical user interface (GUI)

One form in common use is the graphical user interface or GUI system (pronounced 'Gooey'). Small pictures or icons representing actions are displayed and can be selected with the mouse. The use of windows makes the operation of programs easier.

Sometimes the menu choices appear 'grey' or 'ghosted' and cannot be selected, for example, the Paste command in the Edit menu cannot be used until data has been passed to the clipboard using the Cut or Copy commands.

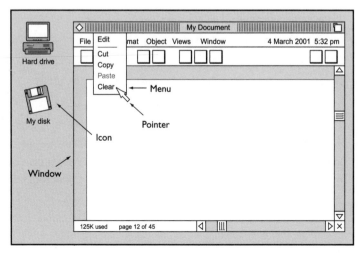

The screen may display several windows for different applications but only the one currently in use will be active. Another term used for this form of interface is WIMP (windows, icons, menus and pointer).

Command line interface

It is possible to give the computer instructions without the aid of menus and icons. (To leave Windows, choose the MS-DOS prompt in the Start, Programs menu.) This is done by typing the instructions directly into the computer so that they can be seen onscreen. This has the disadvantage that the user must know the commands to type in. The advantage is that quite specific instructions can be given directly.

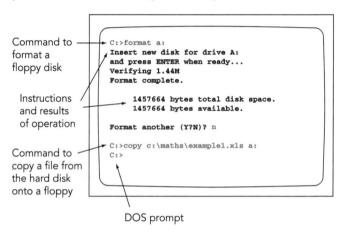

Command to format a floppy disk

Instructions and results of operation

Command to copy a file from the hard disk onto a floppy

```
C:>format a:
Insert new disk for drive A:
and press ENTER when ready...
Verifying 1.44M
Format complete.

    1457664 bytes total disk space.
    1457664 bytes available.

Format another (Y?N)? n

C:>copy c:\maths\example1.xls a:
C:>
```

DOS prompt

Questions

1 A package is described as 'mouse-driven'.

   a Explain what this term means.

   ....

   b State two features you would expect to find when using the package.

   ....

   ....

2 In graphical user interfaces, the choices available in the drop-down menus are 'greyed' or 'ghosted' out and cannot be selected. Explain why this might occur and give an example.

   ....

   ....

9 Software packages

Software is the name given to computer programs. The table below shows some of the most important programs used in business, schools and at home.

Word processing	
Example uses	Writing letters, reports, projects, books, memos, essays
Example software	Microsoft® Word, WordPerfect
Desktop publishing (DTP)	
Example uses	Leaflets, brochures, posters, advertisements, magazines, newspapers
Example software	Microsoft® Publisher, Adobe PageMaker
Presentation package	
Example uses	Giving presentations, lectures, lessons, assemblies, talks
Example software	Microsoft® PowerPoint
Database	
Example uses	Use to store, sort, search and retrieve information, eg details of customers, telephone directories, product details
Example software	Microsoft® Access, PinPoint
Spreadsheet	
Example uses	Working with numbers, calculations, forecasting, business accounts, mathematical models
Example software	Microsoft® Excel, Lotus 1-2-3
Graphics packages	
Example uses	Drawing and painting pictures, manipulating images, designing graphics
Example software	Microsoft® Paint, CorelDRAW
Computer aided design (CAD)	
Example uses	Technical drawing for design of parts and systems, scale drawing with dimensions
Example software	AutoCAD

The following sections show how these programs operate and some of the features contained in them. The way the different packages are used is illustrated in the example below for a school uniform shop.

The uniform shop purchases the different clothes (blazers, shirts, trousers, ties, sportswear, etc) from the manufacturers.

Garment:	Blazer	**Reference number:**	BL28
Size:	28"	**Number in stock:**	18
Gender:	M & F	**Reorder quantity:**	12

DATABASE
The database holds details of all the goods held in the shop including the type of garment, the size and the number in stock. Daily printed reports of stock levels help in re-ordering items before the shop runs out.

WORD PROCESSOR
Used to write to parents, place orders with the suppliers and prepare the price lists each term.

DESKTOP PUBLISHING
Used to produce brochures and posters advertising the shop and the days and times it opens.

School Uniform Shop

PRESENTATION PACKAGE
Used as part of a presentation evening to parents with children moving up to the secondary school.

GRAPHICS PACKAGE
Used to create and design the graphics used in the uniform shop brochure and the presentation.

SPREADSHEET
Used to calculate the selling price for each item and work out the monthly and yearly sales figures.

Monthly Sales

Word processing

A word processor can be used to write letters, reports, essays, projects, memos, curriculum vitae, theses – in fact, any form of written work. When text is entered at the keyboard, the characters and words are displayed on the screen and held in the computer's memory. This work can be saved to disk and printed.

The advantage of using a word processor is that the text can be changed (edited) onscreen and reprinted if mistakes are made. The word processor also has many features which can be used to format the document.

Formatting

When we format a document we choose the way it looks. Characters can be **bold**, *italic*, <u>underlined</u> or CAPITAL letters. The spacing between letters and lines can be altered or the writing can be set out in columns or tables.

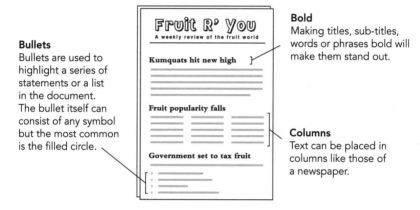

Bullets
Bullets are used to highlight a series of statements or a list in the document. The bullet itself can consist of any symbol but the most common is the filled circle.

Bold
Making titles, sub-titles, words or phrases bold will make them stand out.

Columns
Text can be placed in columns like those of a newspaper.

Fonts

Font is the name we give to styles of print. There are many different fonts. Two quite common ones are Times and Helvetica:

Thickness (line weights) vary considerably

Clearly visible serifs

No serifs

Thickness more consistent

A serif font

A sans serif (without serif) font

Fonts can be broadly grouped into serif and sans serif fonts. Serifs on a character are the cross-strokes that cap the strokes which make up a character. In the illustration on the previous page you can see that the Times font has serifs but the Helvetica font does not. Serifs help the eye flow along the line as the words are read and serif fonts are often used in newspapers and magazines. Sans serif fonts can be used on application forms, for example, where the eye of the reader needs to be drawn to each box in turn.

Justification

There are four ways in which text can lie in a column and at any stage the user can alter all or part of the document to any one of the four. These are illustrated below.

For justification, where the text is lined up to both the left- and right-hand edges, the program checks, line by line, the length of the text. If it is less than the line length, it stretches the text by spreading the letters and words, or by inserting additional spaces.

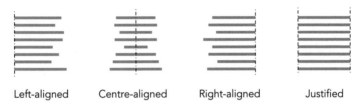

| Left-aligned | Centre-aligned | Right-aligned | Justified |

Tabs

Tabs are often used for setting out tables or columns. Tab positions can be set across the page. Then, when the tab key on the keyboard is pressed, the cursor (flashing bar) will jump to the next tab position across the page.

The four most common types of tab markers – left, right, centre and decimal – are shown below:

Centre tab	Left tab	Right tab	Decimal tab
↓	⌊	⊐↓	↓
Resistor	0.22 ohms	6z – 0100	£0.12
Capacitor	56 pF	08 – 0495	£0.07
Relay	5V DC 80R	60 – 585	£1.10
Semiconductor	3A+5V	LM 323 K	£2.40
Tools	Precision Drill	85 – 55	£29.70

Style sheets

A style sheet holds information about the parts of a document: the body of the text, chapter titles, headings and subheadings, footers and headers, etc. Each style sheet might contain information on the font to be used, the size, alignment, spacings, colour, background, border, shading, etc. Once style sheets have been set up for a document, they are very easy to apply. Highlight the particular text, eg a heading, then select the heading style from the menu list. The advantages of using style sheets in documents are:

- it is quick to apply a range of formatting to the highlighted text

- with long documents, it makes it easy to be consistent, ie all the titles, subtitles, etc having the same style throughout the document

- marking text with the heading style will allow the word processor to create a 'contents' page automatically in longer documents

- it makes it very easy to change formats throughout the whole document.

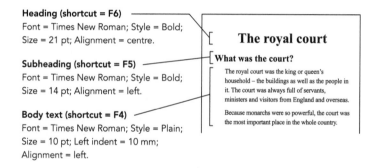

A typical style sheet set-up

Setting up a page

Landscape or portrait

Ordinary A4 paper (29.7 cm x 21 cm) can be printed in two orientations, known as portrait and landscape. As shown below, portrait is printed with the longest side vertical, this is the usual (default) setting. Alternatively, landscape can be selected which prints with the longest side horizontally. Landscape orientation can be useful when designing an A5 booklet where the A4 page will be folded, or for wide tables, illustrations and use of columns.

Portrait   Landscape

Headers

Headers allow the user to specify text which will automatically be printed at the top of each page. The position across the page, and the style and size of the header text, can be specified. Items that might be placed in a header include the description of the document or the chapter number.

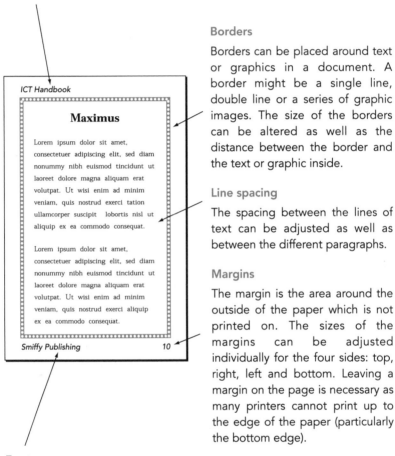

Borders

Borders can be placed around text or graphics in a document. A border might be a single line, double line or a series of graphic images. The size of the borders can be altered as well as the distance between the border and the text or graphic inside.

Line spacing

The spacing between the lines of text can be adjusted as well as between the different paragraphs.

Margins

The margin is the area around the outside of the paper which is not printed on. The sizes of the margins can be adjusted individually for the four sides: top, right, left and bottom. Leaving a margin on the page is necessary as many printers cannot print up to the edge of the paper (particularly the bottom edge).

Footers

A footer, as the name implies, is found at the foot of the page. As with headers, once the layout of a footer is defined for all or part of a document, it will appear on each printed page. The footer often contains the page number which is automatically increased through the document.

Editing

Spell-check

A useful facility for many people! The 'spell-check' makes use of an extensive dictionary held on the disk. Each word in your document is compared with words in the dictionary and the user is invited to change or ignore words selected by the spell-checker. When words in the document are not found in the dictionary, the spell-checker will suggest words that have similar spellings or that sound similar when spoken.

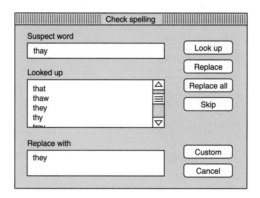

Spell-check box

Often, spell-checkers have the facility to create dictionaries for the user for special words. These words might include real names, address names, postcodes and technical words not normally found in a dictionary. Dictionaries are also available for specialist subjects like medicine.

Grammar check

The grammar check will look at the way each sentence in the document is written and compares it with a set of rules for grammar and style of writing. The user can usually select how strictly these rules are applied to their work. The grammar check will suggest ways in which the sentence can be improved if it varies from the rules. The check often includes statistics on readability: based on the number of syllables in words, the length of words and the number of words in sentences, the reading age can be determined. 'Standard' writing averages 17 words per sentence and 147 syllables per 100 words.

Many modern word processors can check the spelling and grammar as the words are entered, indicating errors with coloured lines.

Thesaurus

This is very useful when you can't think of quite the right word to use in a document. Select a word, or phrase, and the thesaurus will display a range of words with the same or similar meanings. For example, using the phrase 'similar to' in the thesaurus may produce:

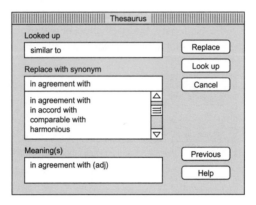

An example of a thesaurus enquiry

Mailmerge

The diagram below illustrates the process of a mailmerge operation. This is often used to produce personalised letters and is achieved by having a standard letter containing fields that pull in data from a separate source. The data source could be a table in a word processor, cells from a spreadsheet or, most commonly, records in a database. When the mailmerge is started, the data replaces the fields in the standard letter. A letter is produced for every database record or row of a table.

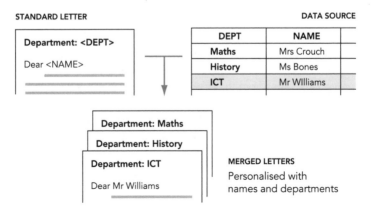

Desktop publishing (DTP)

A desktop publishing (DTP) program allows users to look at the page of the document as a whole and design the layout by marking areas for text and graphics. Text can be typed directly into the DTP package or it can be imported from a word processing package. The text can be arranged in columns with large titles or headlines heading the columns. Images can be imported from graphics packages, scanned, digitised or taken from clip art libraries on the disk or CD-ROM.

All these features can be put together to produce newspapers, newsletters, pages for books, posters, brochures, leaflets, prospectuses, etc.

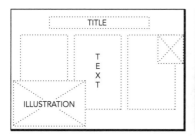   

Design   *Finished page*

Graphics

Documents often require graphics, such as pictures and images, to illustrate the text. These can be imported from:

- clip art libraries supplied with the word processing and DTP packages
- clip art libraries supplied separately on disks
- drawing and painting packages, where images are created by the user
- scanners
- digitisers
- CD-ROMs
- digital cameras.

Once the image is displayed on the computer screen, the user can manipulate the image by resizing, rotating, shearing and cropping. These terms are explained on the next page.

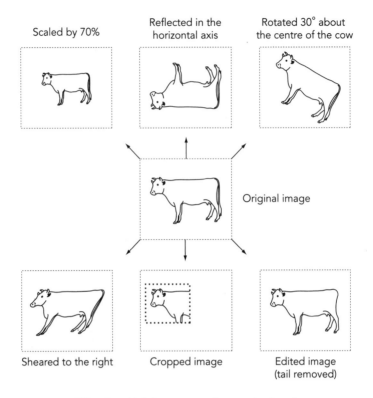

Ways in which images can be manipulated

Layering

When pictures are positioned over text or text is placed over pictures in a document, this is called layering. In order to create the effect required, it may be necessary to select the object and 'Send to back' or 'Bring to front'. It is also possible to make the text background transparent so that the picture or image can be seen behind the text.

Objects in layers can be moved 'on top' of each other

Presentation packages

A presentation package allows users to prepare and give presentations using the computer. The information being presented is made into a set of slides. Each slide can contain text, clip art, graphics, video, sound and animation. A salesman might use the program to demonstrate a new product; a teacher, to give a lesson or lecture; and a pupil might use the software to prepare a talk or a school assembly. Microsoft® PowerPoint is a popular presentation software package that comes with Word and Excel as part of the Microsoft® Office programs.

Preparing the presentation

Before starting work on the computer, it is a good idea to draft out the ideas for each slide of the presentation on paper. When this has been done, the user can choose the best slide layout and design for each slide from a selection offered in the program. Text, graphics, sound and animation are then added to complete the slide.

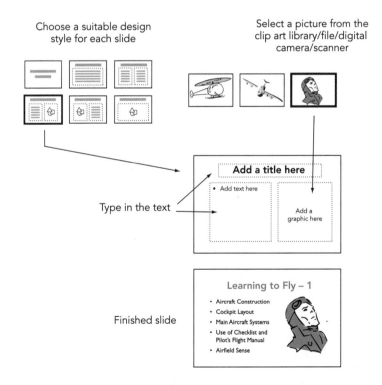

Choose a suitable design style for each slide

Select a picture from the clip art library/file/digital camera/scanner

Add a title here
• Add text here
Add a graphic here

Type in the text

Finished slide

Learning to Fly – 1
• Aircraft Construction
• Cockpit Layout
• Main Aircraft Systems
• Use of Checklist and Pilot's Flight Manual
• Airfield Sense

The amount of text on each slide needs to be quite small; only the key points should be shown. This is so that the writing can be displayed in a large font that is clearly visible to the audience. If more detail needs to be given to the audience, then this can be added as notes and printed out, with a copy of the slide, for the audience to take away after the presentation.

Animation

Animation helps to make more of an impact with the audience. In Microsoft® PowerPoint, the change from one slide to the next can be animated in over 40 different ways. For example, the new slide can appear by wiping across the old slide from the side or bottom. This can be accompanied by selected sounds. Once a slide is on the screen, the text and graphics can be made to appear through animation. Words and pictures can 'drive' in or 'fly' onto the slide. Individual letters can be projected onto the slide as if by a laser beam or appear as if they were printed by a typewriter.

Business use

It is quite common for business people to have to make presentations. These might be to customers, clients or to others in the company. The presentation package can assist the user by offering complete sets of slides for different types of presentation. The user then only has to edit the detail on each slide for their own product or company. Slide sets in Microsoft® PowerPoint include:

- Business plans
- Company meetings
- Flyers
- Marketing meetings
- Organisation structures
- Sales presentations
- Technical product presentations.

Databases

A database is a collection of related data items, which are structured and linked so that the data can be accessed in a number of ways.

A simple database consists of only one set of data. This is called a flat file. An example of a flat file database is PinPoint or Microsoft® Works.

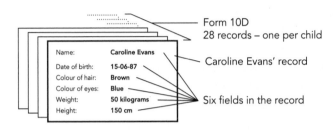

Name:	**Caroline Evans**	
Date of birth:	**15-06-87**	
Colour of hair:	**Brown**	
Colour of eyes:	**Blue**	
Weight:	**50 kilograms**	
Height:	**150 cm**	

Form 10D
28 records – one per child

Caroline Evans' record

Six fields in the record

A relational database is more complex (see page 55). Relational databases are very powerful as they allow the data to be accessed in many different ways. An example of a relational database is Microsoft® Access. On larger commercial systems, there will be many users accessing the data at the same time and examples of these relational databases include Oracle and SQL Server.

Functions of a database

A database program on a computer is designed to hold information (data). Often the amount of information stored is very large and it would take a long time for us to search through this information if it were written on paper. Holding the information in a database enables us to search very quickly and to sort the information easily. The required data can then be printed out as a report.

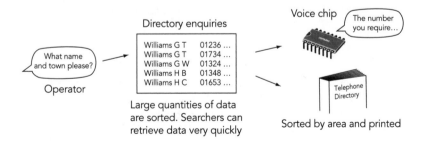

What name and town please?

Operator

Directory enquiries

Williams G T	01236 ...
Williams G T	01734 ...
Williams G W	01324 ...
Williams H B	01348 ...
Williams H C	01653 ...

Large quantities of data are sorted. Searchers can retrieve data very quickly

Voice chip

The number you require...

Telephone Directory

Sorted by area and printed

An example database

Suppose we wished to create a books database. Each student in the class is asked to bring in details of ten books from home. These details will then be added to the class database. Using this database, we could examine the selection of books to determine the:

- most popular publisher
- most popular author
- average number of pages
- average number of chapters
- average number of pages per chapter
- average cost of the books
- most/least popular books.

Typical information for a book might include:

> *The Worst Witch All At Sea* is written by Jill Murphy and published by Penguin. Its ISBN is 0 670 83253 7. It costs £8.99, has 21 chapters and 222 pages. I thought it was excellent and gave it a rating of 9 out of 10.

In our computer database each book would make up a record. Within the record, the details of the book are structured into fields (see page 50).

Title	The Worst Witch All At Sea		
Author	Jill Murphy		
Price	£8.99	Publisher	Penguin
Pages	222	ISBN	0 670 83253 7
Chapters	21	Rating/10	9
Comment	Excellent		

Structuring the data in this way enables the database program to search, sort, display and print the data easily. With the data now contained in specific fields, if we wished to search for the book with the most pages we would instigate a search of the 'Pages' field in each record throughout the database. Structuring the data also enables us to see if a field is empty and whether or not important information is missing.

Sorting

Being able to sort the data is an important function of a database package. The steps involved in sorting data are listed below:

Example

1 Select the field you wish to use to sort by; this might be a 'Surname' field or 'Account number' field. Sometimes you may wish to choose a secondary field to sort by. For example, if the main sort is by surname, a secondary sort would be by first name in case there were several people with the same surname.

2 Decide whether the list should be in ascending ('A' at the top and 'Z' at the bottom) or descending order.

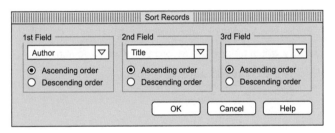

Here the instructions given to the database are to do a main sort by author and a secondary sort by the title of the book

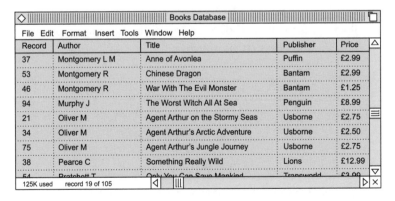

The data is now sorted by author and then title

Note: When you do a sort, numbers come before letters and, depending on the database software, lower case letters come before uppercase letters.

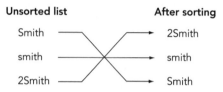

Unsorted list	After sorting
Smith	2Smith
smith	smith
2Smith	Smith

Searching

To be able to retrieve information from a database, particularly from a large database, is vitally important. This is done by the computer taking the user's request and searching for a match in the database. The steps necessary to carry out a search are:

1   Choose the 'query' or 'find' option.

2   Specify which field in the record you wish to search.

3   Decide the condition statement, eg:
> 'is equal to'
> 'is greater than'
> 'is not equal to'
> 'is less than or equal to'
> 'is greater than or equal to'
> 'contains'.

4   Enter the value to be searched for.

5   If another condition needs to be applied to the search, go back to step 2; otherwise start the search.

Example

1   If we were searching the books database to find a book with either 'witches' or 'wizards' in the title, we might use the following search:

Title 'contains' "Witch"

OR

Title 'contains' "Wizard"

Note: The use of the condition 'contains' will find titles that include "Witch", "Witches", "Witchcraft", etc.

2 To search for a highly rated (rating of 10) and cheap book (£5 or less) we might use the search:

Rating 'is equal to' 10
AND
Price 'is less than or equal to' 5

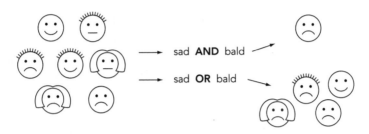

How the AND and OR criteria work

The words AND and OR used between different search statements are called Boolean operators.

Database forms

When you are entering data into a database, you can design the layout by placing boxes and labels onto the screen where the data is to be typed into the different fields. These data input screens are often referred to as forms.

Database reports

Database reports can be designed by the user to show the data or, more usually, print out data from the database. When creating a report, the user can choose whether all or just some of the fields in the database record are to be printed. Data can be printed in columns and number fields can be totalled at the bottom of each page and at the end of the report.

Macros

Databases, along with other packages, have a facility to store a sequence of keystrokes and instructions. These commands are stored as a macro. When the instructions need to be 'replayed', the macro holding the instructions is run. Macros can reduce the time taken for repetitive tasks or make complex instructions simple to perform. For example, in a database, instructions could be stored that would search for certain records, sort them into order and print out the results. The macro containing these instructions could then be activated when the user clicks on a screen button with the mouse.

Database fields

Each record of a database contains fields where the data or information is stored. When a new database is being designed, many database packages request the user to specify the type of data that will be entered into each of the fields. This allows the computer to process the data effectively and allocate computer memory efficiently.

Different types of field include:

- Text field – letters or numbers, eg 'Car registration' = V741GEV

- Number field – numbers which can be used for statistics or calculations. Number fields can be divided further into 'integer' fields (numbers without decimal places) and 'real' numbers (with decimal places). For example, 'Age' = 15 or 'Price' = 12.95.

- Data/time field – these fields are specifically designed to store dates and times which can then be displayed in different formats, eg 2 April 1952 might be displayed in the form:

d-mmmm-yyyy	= 2 April 1952
dd-mmm-yy	= 02-Apr-52
dd-mm-yy	= 02-04-52

  Holding dates in a date field allows searches to take place, eg show records where 'Last payment date' is greater than 1 November 2000.

- Boolean or logical field – in these fields only a 'Yes' or 'No' value will be accepted or a 'True' or 'False' value. For example, 'Has the membership been paid?'.

- Memo field – this is similar to a text field in that it can hold letters and numbers. Memo fields are used when larger amounts of data are entered into the field. 64 000 characters are allowed in Microsoft® Access, whereas the maximum number of characters allowed in a text field is 255.

- Calculation field – this is used when the field displays a calculation based on numbers in other fields. For example, 'Area of circle' = 3.142 x ('Radius field')^2.

- Picture/image field – Many modern databases now have a field where pictures can be displayed within the record. The data entered into this field by the user would include file details of the image to be displayed.

Coding information

It is sometimes useful to code information in database fields. Say, for example, we were entering subjects studied at school, we might code these as:

MA = Maths   EN = English
FR = French   DT = Design and Technology

Advantages:

- easier and quicker to enter

- less typing required

- less likely to make spelling mistakes

- uses less computer memory.

Designing a database table

When creating a new database, is it usual to make a list of the fields needed. For each field, decide what type of field it will be. For example, a field for names will be a text field and a field for a person's age will be a number field.

Be careful with some fields that appear to be number fields but should actually be text fields. Telephone numbers fall into this category. If this field is chosen as a number field, the leading zero at the start of the area code may be removed and any space included between the code and the number may cause an error.

For number fields, decide if the decimal places are required. If the numbers will not have decimal places then choose 'Integer' (or 'Long integer' if numbers over 65536 are to be used). If they do have decimal places, decide how many decimal places are needed. For text fields, decide on the maximum number of characters that field is likely to need. For example, you might choose 25 characters for the first line of an address. On early databases it was a problem if this figure turned out to be too small for the data in some records but in modern databases the user can return to the design screen and increase the field length.

The table on the right shows the design of the fields for the books database shown on page 46.

(A fourth column is often added to this table to show any validation rules that might be applied to the data – see page 53.)

Field name	Type	Length
Title	Text	35
Author	Text	25
Publisher	Text	25
Cost	Currency (2 dp)	
Pages	Number (integer)	
Chapters	Number (integer)	
ISBN	Text	15
Rating	Number (integer)	
Comment	Memo	

Key fields

The key field is the one used to identify each record and is often used when searching and sorting the records. If the record contains a field like an account number and this is a unique number only for that record, then this field is called the primary key field. If there is not a unique primary key, the key field can be formed from several fields, eg 'First address line' and 'Postcode'. This is called a composite key. The primary key for the table shown above could be the ISBN number as this is unique (different) for each book.

Information and data

The two words 'information' and 'data' often seem to mean the same thing. We put information into computers which is stored as data. There is, however, a subtle difference between the two. If, for example, the data in a computer was '02041952', what would this mean? Is it a part number? An account number? A telephone number? If you know it is a date, then you can understand it means 2 April 1952.

Information = Data + 'The context and structure of the data'

Data capture

If we are going to search and sort data in a database, then it is necessary to 'capture' the data first. This can be done using any of the input devices mentioned in *Chapter 3*, although some are more commonly used than others.

Using a questionnaire to gather data and entering this via the keyboard is still one of the most common methods.

Validation

This is the name given to the checks a computer can carry out when data is input. Whatever form of input device is used, some form of check can be made on the data entering the computer.

Example: A database field in a secondary school timetable package contains information about the teacher, subject and year group. This information is coded as follows:

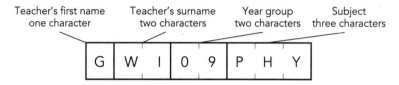

Teacher's first name one character   Teacher's surname two characters   Year group two characters   Subject three characters

| G | W | I | 0 | 9 | P | H | Y |

This shows the code entered for Mr G Williams teaching Physics to Year 9. Here are some checks to make sure that the data has been entered correctly:

Presence check: The field cannot be left empty when completing the record.

⚠ You have not entered a year group code. This field must contain data.
[OK]

Character count: There should always be eight characters in this field; more or fewer would prompt the user to edit the data.

| G | W | I | 0 | 9 | P | | |

Range check: The fourth and fifth characters are extracted from the code and converted to a number. The validation check then ensures that the number is 'equal to or greater than' 7 AND 'less than or equal to' 13 (assuming the school has a sixth form).

$$7 \leq 09 \leq 13 \ ?$$
✓

Table (or file) lookup: Here the teacher's code (first three characters) and the subject code (last three characters) can be checked by opening separate files and ensuring the codes do exist in a valid list.

G WILLIAMS ✓

GWI

Picture check: This checks that the data entered in this field is as expected, ie TTTNNTTT (where T = text and N = number).

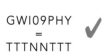

GWI09PHY
=
TTTNNTTT   ✓

There are also a number of totalling checks that can be carried out when processing data. Take, for example, a payroll program which is run at the end of each month to calculate the wages. The hours worked by each employee are input to disk in preparation for running the payroll program. At the front of the data, in a batch header record, several extra pieces of information can be included. These enable the computer program to check the data being entered and report any errors. This data includes:

- Batch totals – how many records are being processed
- Control totals – a manually calculated figure, eg the total hours worked
- Hash totals – a total, often quite meaningless, figure calculated by the computer, eg the sum of all the employee numbers.

These checks help ensure that the program processes the payroll accurately and that no employees are left out or are paid incorrectly.

Check digits

Some numbers are given an extra digit on the end which is called a check digit. This digit is calculated from the original number and acts as a check when the number is read by the computer. There are several ways in which these check digits are calculated. One popular method is called the modulus-11 method. An example of how the check digit is calculated is shown below:

1. Multiply each digit in the number by a factor, starting with two and going up by one.

Original number	1	2	3	4
	x	x	x	x
Multiply factors	5	4	3	2

2. Add the products together

$$5 + 8 + 9 + 8 = 30$$

3. Divide the total by 11

$30 \div 11 = 2$ remainder 8

4. Subtract the remainder from 11 to obtain the check digit*.

$11 - 8 = 3$ (check digit)

The new number, including its check digit becomes **1234 3**

*There are two special cases; if the remainder is '1', the check digit is 'X'. If the remainder is '0', the check digit is '0'.

When the computer reads the number (including the check digit), it checks the calculation and gives an error message if it is not correct. This procedure traps 99% of common errors like getting two digits mixed up.

Numbers that use check digits include customer account numbers, International Standard Book Numbers (ISBNs) and the numbers on bar codes. You may have noticed at the checkout till of the supermarket that some products have to be passed several times across the scanner before the beep tells the assistant it has been read correctly. Each time a product is scanned, the number associated with the black and white lines is validated using the check digit.

Relational databases

The type of database shown earlier in this section is called a flat file database. The data is held in a single file and the sorting, searching and printing of reports is done on this datafile. This sort of database is suitable for use at home or in a school but it would not be adequate for larger businesses and organisations. Here a large amount of data is required and it is necessary to separate the data into tables with each table holding data relating to one subject or entity.

In relational databases, the tables of data exist independently from the programs which may use them. The database management system (DBMS) provides the software tools to link the tables together and do searches of the data. Each user may have a different view of the database, with restricted data only being accessible to those with the necessary authority. Different departments and individuals can be given permission to edit and update parts of the data. For example, the sales department may be given the task of ensuring that the customer data is kept up-to-date.

Customer details

Customer Number	Customer Name	Postcode	Tel
10223	Kocher J	CM4 3FF	01245 .....
15333	Ridley S	CO4 2WS	01206 .....
12133	Castle B	CM2 1RW	01245 .....
14277	Hunt S	CO2 1JJ	01206 .....

Relationship between tables

Orders received

Order Number	Customer Number	Date	Total Cost
8143	10223	06-06-00	£12.32
8144	15333	07-06-00	£21.16
8145	10223	07-06-00	£9.00
8146	14277	07-06-00	£40.95

Database Management System

In relational databases, data is grouped into tables

Questions

1 Mr Yap is a dentist and keeps records of his patients in a database so that he can send out reminder letters every six months. Which of the following fields would be included?

   a ☐ Date of last appointment

   b ☐ Patient's address

   c ☐ How much the patient earns

   d ☐ Type of car the patient drives

2 Complete the following sentences by inserting the correct word from the list given below:

   file   fields   key   customer   unique

   "There is one record for each .... on the bank's customer

   database .... Each record consists of ....

   giving details of the customer. Each customer is given a

   .... account number with the bank; this is called the

   .... field."

3 The third set of Physics pupils is taught by Mr G Williams and is coded in a database as:

   • First three letters of the subject

   • A number for the set

   • First letter of the teacher's first name

   • First two letters of the teacher's surname

   The code is: PHY3GWI

   What is the code for the following groups:

   a The second Geography set with Mrs F Long? ....

   b The first Art class with Miss E McVeigh? ....

   c Give one reason why codes are used in databases.

   ....

4 A company adds a record to a datafile whenever it sells to a new customer. State one validation check that could be used when the number of the month of first sale is entered.

   ....

Spreadsheets

A spreadsheet is a computer program which is designed to display and process numbers. It is made up of a grid into which numbers are entered. The program contains many mathematical, statistical and financial calculations which can be applied to the numbers. Many spreadsheets can also show the numbers in the form of graphs.

A spreadsheet is a powerful tool for experimenting with different mathematical models and asking 'What if...?' (see page 59). For example, the manager of a supermarket needs to know how many checkout tills to open at different times of the day. If too many tills are open, then staff are sitting idle and the store is wasting money. If too few are open, long queues develop and customers become cross because they have to wait a long time. Based on the number of customers in the store and the average time each customer spends at the checkout, a spreadsheet model will tell the manager the ideal number of tills to open.

Spreadsheet cells

Cells in the spreadsheet may contain numbers, text (letters, words, etc), dates and formulae. Each cell, or a block of cells, may be 'formatted' so that the contents of the cell is displayed in different ways.

The table below shows some of the different ways numbers can be formatted in the cells of a spreadsheet. This example shows how the number 12345.6789 would be displayed in the various formats:

Format	Example	Description
0	12346	integer
0.00	12345.68	2 decimal places
#,##0	12,346	integer with thousands separator
£0.00	£12345.68	pounds and pence

Calculations

The power of a spreadsheet comes from its ability to do calculations with numbers. The contents of one cell can be calculated from other cells in the sheet.

		A	B	C	D	
1		length	width	area		
2		4	3	→ 12		
3						
4						

125K used   Cell B4

Formula   =A2*B2.

Sometimes when students see this kind of spreadsheet they want to type the answer '12' straight into cell C2. However, cell C2 should contain =A2*B2. If the number in cell A2 or B2 is now changed, the new area will automatically be calculated in cell C2.

Formulae and functions

Spreadsheet packages come with a library of formulae and functions as part of the program. There are formulae for financial calculations, for handling dates and times, for mathematical and statistical work and for logical expressions. In the example below, two of the many functions are illustrated – the SUM function and the IF statement.

An example of using a function to show the results of an examination is given below. The pass mark is 40% and the formulae in the right-hand column show whether the student has passed or failed.

	A	B	C	D	E	F	G
1			Paper 1	Paper 2	Paper 3	Total	PASS/
2			(30%)	(30%)	(40%)	(%)	FAIL
3	Katie-Marie	NORMAN	12	14	20	=SUM(C3:E3)	=IF(F3>39,"PASS", "FAIL")
4	Noel	LUFF	4	5	15	=SUM(C4:E4)	=IF(F4>39,"PASS", "FAIL")
5	Catherine	OAKLEY	15	19	27	=SUM(C5:E5)	=IF(F5>39,"PASS", "FAIL")
6	Laura	ODD	9	13	30	=SUM(C6:E6)	=IF(F6>39,"PASS", "FAIL")
7	Matthew	LAWRIE	13	9	17	=SUM(C7:E7)	=IF(F7>39,"PASS", "FAIL")

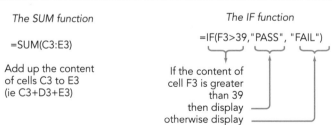

The SUM function

=SUM(C3:E3)

Add up the content
of cells C3 to E3
(ie C3+D3+E3)

The IF function

=IF(F3>39,"PASS", "FAIL")

If the content of
cell F3 is greater
than 39
then display
otherwise display

	A	B	C	D	E	F	G
1			Paper 1	Paper 2	Paper 3	Total	PASS/
2			(30%)	(30%)	(40%)	(%)	FAIL
3	Katie-Marie	NORMAN	12	14	20	46	PASS
4	Noel	LUFF	4	5	15	24	FAIL
5	Catherine	OAKLEY	15	19	27	61	PASS
6	Laura	ODD	9	13	30	52	PASS
7	Matthew	LAWRIE	13	9	17	39	FAIL

'What if...?'

'What if...?' is a phrase often associated with spreadsheets. If a number in one cell is changed, then the value in another cell may also change since it uses the first number in a calculation. The second cell may change a third cell, and so on through the sheet. The values in your spreadsheet model can be recalculated instantly when you change the contents of individual cells to investigate, for example, "What if the price is increased to...?" "What if the sales fall by...?" "What if the VAT rate changes to...?", etc.

Constructing a spreadsheet

The sheet below shows the sales from the school tuck shop for a week:

	A	B	C	D	E	F
1		Crisps	Mars bars	Snickers	Apples	
2	Mon	17	22	12	11	
3	Tue	23	19	7	14	
4	Wed	24	16	8	9	
5	Thu	18	17	9	11	
6	Fri	21	16	13	12	
7	Total sold					
8						
9	Sale price	25	30	25	20	
10	Cost price	20	24	18	10	
11						
12	Total sales					
13	Total costs					
14						
15	Weekly profit					

1 In column F, we can total the number of items sold each day. In cell F2, we would use the formula =SUM(B2:E2). After entering this, cell F2 would display the answer 62. To insert this calculation for Tuesday to Friday in cells F3 to F6, we copy or replicate the calculation from F2.

2 In row 7, we can total the individual items sold during the week. In cell B7, we would enter the formula =SUM(B2:B6). We would then copy this formula into cells C7 to E7.

3   To find how much money or income we have made from the sales of each item, we need to add a formula to the cells in row 12. In B12, the formula is =B7*B9; this will work out how much money we have made during the week from the sale of crisps.

4   The items sold at the tuck shop need to be purchased by the school. Row 10 of the sheet shows the cost for each item. In row 13, we need to show the total costs for the items sold during the week. The formula for this is =B7*B10.

	A	B	C	D	E	F
1		Crisps	Mars bars	Snickers	Apples	
2	Mon	17	22	12	11	62
3	Tue	23	19	7	14	63
4	Wed	24	16	8	9	57
5	Thu	18	17	9	11	55
6	Fri	21	16	13	12	62
7	Total sold	103	90	49	57	
8						
9	Sale price	25	30	25	20	
10	Cost price	20	24	18	10	
11						
12	Total sales	2575	2700	1225	1140	
13	Total costs	2060	2160	882	570	
14						
15	Weekly profit	515	540	343	570	

5   The profit is the difference between the selling price and the buying price. Therefore, the formula needed for row 15 is =B12-B13.

6   Our final task is to copy the formulae in B12, B13 and B15 across the sheet.

Note: All of the money values in the sheet are shown in pence. It would be easier to show the larger numbers in rows 12, 13 and 15 in pounds. This can be done in two steps:

7   Divide by 100 to change pence into pounds.

8   Format the cells to currency to show the £ sign.

	A	B	C	D	E	F
12	Total sales	£25.75	£27.00	£12.25	£11.40	
13	Total costs	£20.60	£21.60	£8.82	£5.70	
14						
15	Weekly profit	£5.15	£5.40	£3.43	£5.70	

Question

A spreadsheet is used to help manage the stock in a car accessories shop. Part of this spreadsheet is shown below:

	A	B	C	D
1	Description	Unit Cost	Quantity	
2				
3	Cans of oil	6.50	40	260.00
4	Bottles of antifreeze	4.00	25	100.00
5	Tool kits	14.50	45	652.50
6	Car jacks	24.00	18	432.00
7				
8			Total value =	1444.50

a Write out the formula in D8 that will work out the value shown.

....

b Other than the cells containing a formula, give examples of two other forms of information that have been typed into the sheet.

  i Type: .... Cell address: ....

  ii Type: .... Cell address: ....

c It has been decided to reduce the stock levels to £1000. Explain how the spreadsheet could be used to help do this.

....

....

d Complete the sentences using words from the list given below:

> copied   C5   A1   formatted   D5   D8
> A5   formula   what   if   bold   B3

"The cells in columns B and D have been .... to display

the numbers to two decimal places. Cell D3 contains a

.... and this has been .... into cells D4, D5

and D6. If the unit cost for the tool kits were to change in cell B5,

this would change the values in .... and ...."

Computer graphics

Generating graphics on the computer has many different and important uses. Drawing and painting packages can be used by illustrators to create images, and games programmers use graphics extensively to produce fast and exciting animations. Many of the special effects seen on television have been generated through computer graphics, and computer aided design (CAD) is vital for many businesses (see next page).

Clip art

Programs, like the Microsoft® Office collection, come with their own library of professionally prepared graphics for use in documents and publications. CDs can also be purchased containing different clip art pictures.

Input devices used with drawing and painting packages are the mouse, scanners (digitisers) and graphics tablets (see pages 6 to 8).

Painting packages

Painting programs such as Microsoft® Paint, which comes with Microsoft® Windows, are always popular. Paint programs are usually raster graphics packages where the image is held as a bitmap. The picture is made up of tiny picture elements called pixels (see page 15).

When you zoom into a bitmap image, the edges are often jagged and it is not always easy to rescale the picture. Bitmap images take up a lot of computer memory as even the blank parts of the picture are stored.

Drawing/illustration packages

Drawing programs, like Microsoft® Draw, use vector graphics. This means that the shapes which are drawn are stored in memory as a series of instructions. This makes them easy to rescale and they take up less memory.

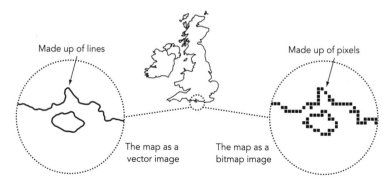

Made up of lines

Made up of pixels

The map as a vector image

The map as a bitmap image

Computer aided design (CAD)

CAD packages are used by scientists, engineers and designers to design many things including cars, bridges, ships, waterways, circuit boards, computers, machinery, dams, chemical plants, oil rigs and buildings. The software needed is often complex and requires powerful computers to run it.

Computer aided design packages have many special features, including:

- allowing the designer to draw an object in two-dimensions (flat) and then having the software build and display a three-dimensional, 'solid' version of the design

- allowing the object to be rotated and viewed from different angles

- 'suggesting' suitable materials for constructing the objects, eg materials with sufficient strength or flexibility

- calculating the stresses and strains that a structure will have to withstand and, where necessary, give warnings of designs that are not safe

- simulating and testing the finished design, eg where CAD is used to design an electronic circuit, it can simulate the operation of the circuit.

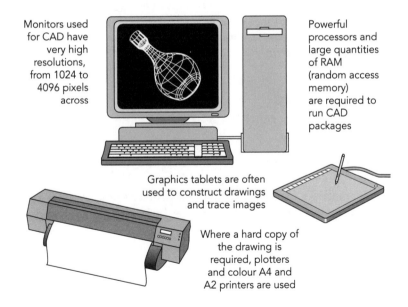

Monitors used for CAD have very high resolutions, from 1024 to 4096 pixels across

Powerful processors and large quantities of RAM (random access memory) are required to run CAD packages

Graphics tablets are often used to construct drawings and trace images

Where a hard copy of the drawing is required, plotters and colour A4 and A2 printers are used

Using CAD software enables drawings to be done more quickly. Changes can be made without having to start the whole drawing again and parts of drawings which are needed more than once can be copied and then duplicated as many times as required. Many companies have large libraries of drawings held on disk which can be retrieved and modified very rapidly. Very fine detail can be achieved by zooming in on the drawing, and the tedious task of shading areas can be done automatically by the computer.

Using a computer network, a number of designers can work on the same project at the same time and workers throughout the company, from the board room to the shop floor, can access drawings on their terminals to assist them with their work and decision making.

Computer aided design software is not just a drawing package. It can be sophisticated software that can calculate, from the dimensions of the drawing, the weight, strains and the stresses that the finished object will endure. In this way, weakness in structures like bridges can be avoided. When using CAD software to design electronic circuits, the software can simulate voltages to test the circuit even before it has been constructed.

Computer aided manufacture (CAM)

Computer aided manufacture is a process of aiding production in manufacturing companies by using computers to operate machines. Some machines shape materials; three of the more common processes are lathing, milling and drilling:

A lathed component

A milled component

A drilled component

Other machines transport the goods between one process and the next, and computer-controlled robot arms may be involved in spraying paint or welding joints.

CAD/CAM

The most effective method of production is to design products using a computer aided design package and then pass instructions directly from this package to the machines able to manufacture the product. Data from the design software is translated into instructions for guiding the lathes, milling and drilling machines. The whole process is fully automated. The introduction of these systems into the manufacturing industry have:

- increased production – machines do not need breaks or sleep
- dramatically reduced the numbers of workers
- reduced the demand for machine operators
- created the demand for skilled computer operators.

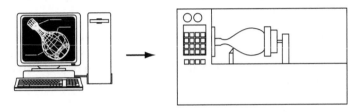

Product is designed on CAD system, the data is transferred to computer numeric control (CNC) machines, and the product manufactured with CAM

Questions

1   What does CAD stand for?

....

2   State three features/facilities you might expect to find on the drawing screen in a computer aided design package.

....

....

....

3   Give two differences between the type of monitor used to produce complex and detailed drawings in CAD and the monitor purchased for use on a home or school computer.

i   ....

ii ....

Modelling and simulation packages

Modelling packages

Modelling is when a computer program attempts to represent a real situation. In order to do this, mathematical equations are used, but the accuracy of the computer model depends on how well the 'real' process is understood. Different values can be input to the model to investigate possible outcomes. A spreadsheet can be used as a modelling program.

Simulation packages

A simulation program is designed to predict the likely behaviour of a real-life system. The real-life situation is represented as a mathematical model in the computer program. Simulation packages include flight simulators and weather forecasting.

Modern flight simulators used for training pilots are full-size cockpits mounted on hydraulic arms to give a full range of movement. Computer screens are positioned in place of windows and these display lifelike images which change according to movement of the aircraft through the controls.

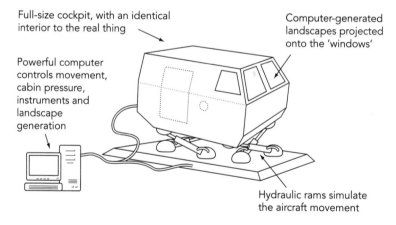

Full-size cockpit, with an identical interior to the real thing

Computer-generated landscapes projected onto the 'windows'

Powerful computer controls movement, cabin pressure, instruments and landscape generation

Hydraulic rams simulate the aircraft movement

To be able to train a pilot in a lifelike simulator without leaving the ground can have a number of advantages. These include:

- the simulator is less expensive to operate than an actual aeroplane
- pilot training is not affected by weather conditions
- training in emergency situations can be safely given
- different conditions such as night flying can be simulated
- practice can be given in take-off and landing at airports worldwide.

Multimedia packages

Multimedia packages consist of text, graphics, sound, animations, photographs, full motion video, hyperlinks, Internet links, questions, puzzles and quizzes. The key feature of a multimedia package is its interactivity; the user can explore by choosing their own route through the package, learning at their own speed.

Multimedia packages offer a wealth of resource material which students can transfer across into their project work. This involves copying the material to the computer's clipboard and then pasting it into their own document. Many multimedia packages contain extensive collections of photographs that can be particularly useful for school projects.

Why multimedia packages are on CD/DVDs

The graphics, audio and video clips contained in multimedia packages use up a lot of memory so it is not possible to distribute programs on floppy disks which only hold 1.4 MB of data. CD-ROMs, which can store up to 650 MB of data, are the most common medium for holding multimedia packages, although even now this amount of storage is insufficient for some titles. One of the versions of the encyclopedia Microsoft® Encarta Reference Suite 2001 is now available on one DVD (see page 26); the equivalent version on CD-ROM requires three discs which need to be swapped in and out of the CD drive as the program is used.

The illustration below shows the amount of multimedia content that can be held on a 650 MB CD-ROM:

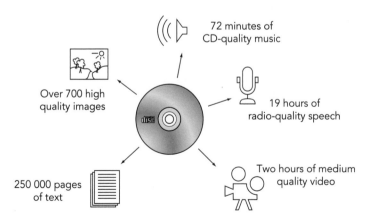

72 minutes of CD-quality music

Over 700 high quality images

19 hours of radio-quality speech

250 000 pages of text

Two hours of medium quality video

10 Data logging

Data logging can be defined as the capture and storage of data for use at a later time. Sensors are used to input the data which is stored in memory. This data can then be displayed in graphs and tables, passed to a spreadsheet program for analysis, and printed and saved on computer disk. Data logging is particularly important in scientific experiments.

Sensors

Almost all physical properties can be measured with sensors. There are sensors to measure light, heat, sound, movement, pressure, radiation, strains and stresses in materials, acidity and humidity. Some of the more common sensors are described in detail in the input devices section (see pages 13 and 14).

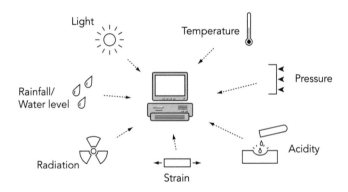

When an experiment is taking place in the laboratory, it is possible to link sensors directly through their control boxes to the computer. If we wish to record data out in the field, equipment would be needed that could measure and store data until the unit is brought to a computer and the data downloaded. Where the recording was taking place would determine how robust the data logging equipment would have to be. For example, if it was recording a river height or the pH level, it would have to be waterproof. In chemical plants, the equipment might have to be resistant to acids and alkalis. Data logging equipment and any onboard computer equipment in a satellite would need to work in a vacuum, with extremes of temperature and radiation.

Using data logging equipment for experiments

There are a number of advantages in using data logging in experiments. These include:

- Data loggers can record measurements with great accuracy.

- Sometimes the very act of taking a reading may interfere with the experiment, eg inserting a thermometer in a liquid may cool the liquid a fraction and also allow heat to escape through a lid. Sensors can be sealed inside the equipment.

- Data loggers can collect data measurements over very short or very long periods of time. For example, equipment could record and process hundreds of measurements during a chemical reaction lasting less than a second. Alternatively, it could be set to record the growth of a plant by taking measurements every hour, day and night, for months or even years.

- Data logging equipment can work reliably and consistently for long periods of time. People would need to take breaks to eat and sleep, and, when tired, their efficiency may be reduced.

- Data loggers can operate in environments which would be hostile to people. Equipment can be designed to operate in orbiting satellites, the depths of the oceans, deserts, or the Arctic or Antarctic.

Analogue and digital

A digital signal consists of pulses of electricity passing along a wire or track of a circuit board. At any point in the signal, there are only two states, either a pulse of electricity is present or there is no pulse. There is no in-between state.

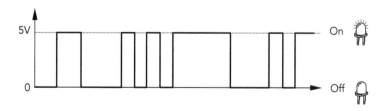

Computers operate using digital signals and all the data and program instructions are coded with different combinations of 1s and 0s.

Many sensors which are used to input data into computers produce analogue signals. Take, for example, a light-dependent resistor (LDR) sensor which reacts to the amount of light falling on it. The resistance to the flow of electricity through the device gets less as the light becomes brighter.

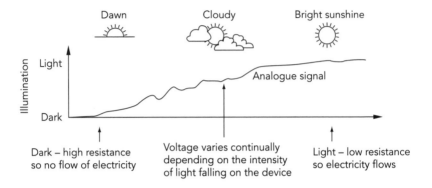

Because computers only work with digital signals, the analogue signals from the sensor must be converted to digital signals. This is done by an electronic device called an 'analogue to digital converter' (or 'A to D converter' for short). The varying voltage of the analogue signal is converted into pulses.

Sometimes it is necessary to reverse this process and take the digital signal from the computer to an output device that needs an analogue signal. In this case a 'digital to analogue converter' (or 'D to A converter') is used.

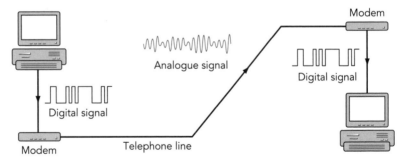

For example, the audio signal that travels along the telephone wire is analogue. A modem (see page 80) is both an 'A to D converter' and a 'D to A converter'. When connecting a computer to the Internet using telephone cables, the modem converts the incoming signals to digital for the computer and the outgoing signals from the computer to analogue to travel along the wires.

Question

In the science experiment shown on the right, the beaker contains a clear liquid. When a second substance is added to the beaker, the two react and the contents of the beaker turn cloudy thus preventing the light from passing through.

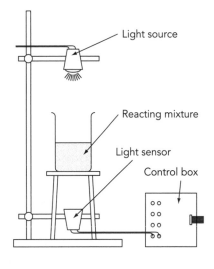

a What electronic component might be used as the light sensor?

....

....

....

b Would the output from the light sensor be an analogue or a digital signal?

....

c What form of signal does the computer require in order to process data – analogue or digital?

....

d Give two reasons why this reaction might be best monitored using the data logging equipment shown.

....

....

....

....

e If instead of the liquid in the beaker going cloudy, the reaction caused the temperature of the liquid to increase, say how you might modify the experiment to monitor this.

....

....

....

11 Computer control

Computers are now used to control the operation of many machines and everyday objects. The instructions contained in the computer program send signals out of the computer to devices like switches and motors which make the machine operate in the correct way.

Embedded computers

When a computer is used to control a machine, the computer circuit board is installed inside the machine. The input sensors and output control devices are then connected to these circuits. This is an embedded computer. The input/output devices that we are most familiar with – the keyboard, mouse and monitor – are not required.

The computer control program is written using a 'normal' computer and 'downloaded' into the embedded computer. The software program is stored in a ROM (read only memory) chip and activates when the machine is switched on.

It is necessary to input data from both the machines and the surrounding environment. The sorts of input and output devices associated with computer control are illustrated below (more detail on these devices is given on pages 5 to 21):

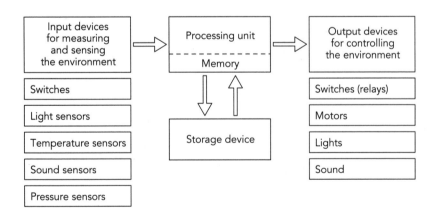

Feedback

Feedback is a term used in computer control when data input from a sensor causes the control program to make changes by sending signals to output devices. These changes are then recorded by the input sensor and data signals sent back to the computer.

This process forms a loop as illustrated in the example below:

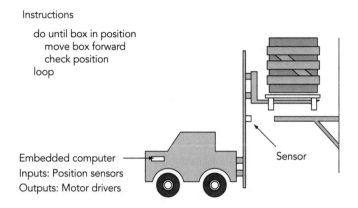

Instructions

    do until box in position
      move box forward
      check position
    loop

Embedded computer
Inputs: Position sensors
Outputs: Motor drivers

Sensor

Machine putting a box onto a shelf in a warehouse

Variables

A computer program needs to be able to examine the data entering and being stored in the processor. A variable is a unit of computer memory that has been given a specific name so that the data held in that memory can be accessed easily by the program. For example, in a washing machine, the data from the heat sensor (thermistor) measuring the water temperature might be held in a variable called 'temp'. The computer program would then monitor the temperature by looking at this variable:

If temp>60 then heater_off

Variable names are chosen by the person writing the program.

Using computers for control

The benefits of using computers for control are as follows:

- Although the cost of computerised machines in factories is high, the operating costs are low in comparison to wages for people doing the job.
- Computers work without the need for breaks and sleep.

- The quality of output from the machine is consistent.

- Machines can handle very heavy work or very precise tasks.

- Machines can work in places that are uncomfortable or hostile for people.

- Computers process data very quickly and so the machines can operate faster.

- Computers can operate the machines with data from a range of sources.

Applications

Some common applications of using computers for control are as follows:

Washing machine

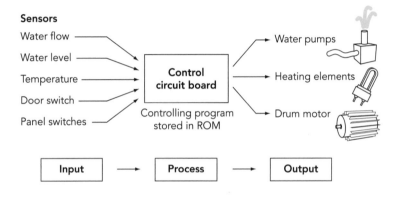

Inputs: Water flow sensors, water level sensors, temperature sensors, panel switches, door open switch, spin speed selector.

Process: Stored programs for different wash cycles, eg woollens, cotton, etc. Each program controls the water temperature and level, and the timing and sequence of the wash, rinse and spin cycles.

Outputs: Switches to operate water pumps and valves, water heaters and the drum motor.

Microwave oven

Inputs: Switches from the key pad, door closed sensor.

Process: Mainly timing processes but also sequences of microwave and grill functions.

Outputs: Switches to control grill and microwave power settings, inside light and buzzer.

Watch

Inputs: Push button switches.

Process: Date, day, time, timer, alarm and stopwatch facilities.

Outputs: LCD screen or hour and minute hands and alarm beeper.

Camera

Inputs: Light sensor, push buttons, film speed sensor, battery power and end of film sensor.

Process: Calculate light level and adjust shutter speed and aperture (size of hole allowing light in) according to film speed. Focus the lens to produce a sharp image. Activate motor to wind film on and draw back shutter for the next picture. Activate flash if necessary.

Outputs: Shutter release switch, motor on/off switch, flash.

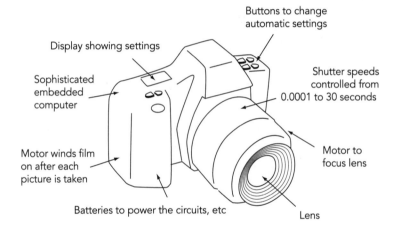

Buttons to change automatic settings

Display showing settings

Sophisticated embedded computer

Shutter speeds controlled from 0.0001 to 30 seconds

Motor winds film on after each picture is taken

Motor to focus lens

Batteries to power the circuits, etc

Lens

Robotic arm

Inputs: Movement coordinates entered at a keyboard or memorised as a skilled worker guides the arm in a learning process, pressure sensors, switches.

Process: Arm follows a pattern of movements held in memory. Switches operate the tools, eg spray painting car bodies on a car manufacturing production line. Sensors on the arm detect and feedback information on its position in relation to the job.

Outputs: Switches to control movement (electric motors, pneumatic valves or hydraulic pumps) and to operate tools being used by the arm.

Question

A car park has automatic entry and exit barriers to allow cars in and out. The computer program that controls these barriers contains a number of variables (memory locations storing data):

Variable	Description
cars_start	the number of cars in the car park at the beginning of the day
cars_in	the number of cars entering the car park
cars_out	the number of cars leaving the car park
max_cars	the maximum number of car parking spaces available

Each time a car enters the car park, the number in 'cars_in' increments (goes up) by one. As a car leaves, the number in 'cars_out' increments by one.

a   Another variable called 'total_cars' is used to hold the total number of cars in the car park at any one time. Show how this can be calculated from the variables above.

....

b   Using the variable 'total_cars', which of the following lines of code would test to see if the entrance barrier should be opened?

☐ If total_cars < max_cars
☐ If total_cars > cars_out
☐ If cars_in – cars_out = zero
☐ If max_cars <cars_start

c   A light beam was used to detect cars entering the car park. As the car broke the beam, a signal was passed to the computer from the light sensor. It was soon found that pedestrians taking a short-cut into the car park through the barrier were triggering the sensor. Describe a better way of detecting the cars entering.

....
....
....
....

12 Communication

A vital part of Information and Communication Technology is for computers to send data to other computers, peripherals and control devices. There are a number of ways in which this data can travel:

Communication with cables

Wire cables

+ Cheap and easy to use
− Signal needs boosting over long distances

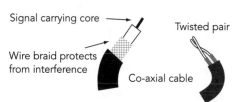

Signal carrying core

Wire braid protects from interference

Co-axial cable

Twisted pair

A common type of cable used for networking computers is called UTP cable. This is likely to be used for your school network and stands for unshielded twisted pair. The cable has eight wires that form four twisted pairs, each with its own colour code so that the network plugs and sockets can be wired correctly.

Fibre-optic cable

+ Can carry many signals at the same time
+ Free from electrical interference
+ Data is secure
+ Does not suffer from corrosion
− Equipment and cables are expensive

Thin glass fibre

A light beam travels through the fibre, carrying the digital signal

Protective sheaths

Communication without cables

Wireless

Connecting a computer to a network using a wireless connection is becoming increasingly popular. A box with a wireless antenna is connected to the network and positioned in a area central to where the computers are to be used. Desktop and notebook computers are then fitted with wireless cards.

+ Can move around with a laptop
+ No need for fixed cables and sockets
− Still quite low bandwidth (slow data transfer)
− Limited range (approximately 100 m)
− Signals absorbed by walls
− Performance decreases as more computers used

Microwave

+ Secure data communication between remote sites
− Direct line of sight required

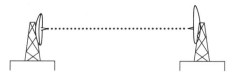

Infra-red

+ Freedom of movement for the machine
− Must have direct line of sight
− May be affected by strong sunlight

Satellite

+ Communication between continents
− Expensive to put satellites in orbit

Satellites use a narrow, highly directional beam capable of many simultaneous transmissions. They are usually in an orbit such that their position above the Earth does not change (called a geostationary orbit).

Short range radio

The latest technology, called Bluetooth, is being developed to link devices without the need for cables or 'line-of-sight' infra-red connections. It uses short range radio waves which can travel up to ten metres. Bluetooth applications include connecting the mouse and keyboard to computers, and wireless headsets to mobile phones.

Local area networks (LANs)

Computer systems are networked when they are linked together. This linking can be through wire cables, fibre-optic cables, microwave links or satellite. When computer systems are linked on the same site, eg a school, this is called a local area network (LAN).

Server

A server is a powerful computer which holds the software to run the network. It also holds the shared resources of the network like the users' files, software packages and printer queues. The advantages of using a network computer are:

- Printers can be shared – individual workstations do not need their own printer. When they print, the data is stored in a queue on the server. The data is then passed to the printer in turn.

- Programs can be shared – software packages are stored on the server and downloaded to workstations as requested.

- Data can be shared – database files stored in the server are available to users around the network; data from CD-ROMs can also be shared.
- Users can communicate with others on the network, sending messages and sharing files.
- There is control over users' access rights to programs and data.

The disadvantages of using a network are:

- The cost of installing the equipment is greater.
- A network manager is needed to run the system.
- If the server fails, all the workstations are affected.
- As data is shared there is a greater need for security.

Network topology

Network topology is the name given to the way in which the computers are connected in the network. Computers can be connected in a bus, star or ring network structure:

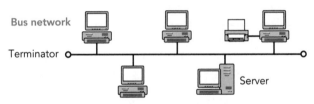

Bus network

Terminator

Server

+ Easy and inexpensive to install (least amount of cable required)
− If the main cable fails, all the computers will be affected
− Performance of the network slows down with more users

Star network

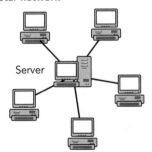

Server

+ Steady high performance, affected less by how many other computers on the network are being used
+ A cable failure does not affect other users
− Uses a lot of cables which is expensive
− Requires a 'hub' box at the file server to control all the cables

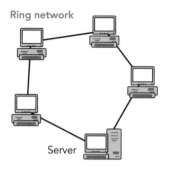

Ring network

+ Data traffic between stations on the network is fast as it flows in one direction only

− If the cable fails, all the workstations are affected

Server

When using a computer on a network, it is necessary to 'log on' using a user name and password. The person responsible for looking after the network is called the network manager. They can give each user access to the particular programs and data they need.

Network cards

In order to connect to a local area network, the computer must have a network card fitted. These cards slot into the main circuit board at the back of the computer enabling data to pass between the computer and network cables. Each card on the network has a unique electronic 'address' that ensures data is delivered correctly. The typical speed at which data is transferred across the network cards is 100 mbps (100 megabits per second) although 10 mbps is still used on older networks.

Wide area networks (WANs)

When computers are linked over larger geographical areas, they form a wide area network (WAN). An example of a wide area network is the Internet which allows computer users to link to other computers around the world, often for the price of a local telephone call. To enable a computer to send and receive data using the telephone line, a modem, ISDN or ADSL connection is required.

Modem

The word 'modem' is short for **mo**dulator **dem**odulator. Modems convert the digital signals in the computer to audio tones which can travel across the telephone system. It also converts incoming signals back into a digital form. The speed at which modems can transmit and receive data varies. The faster the modem, the quicker data transfers will be and lower telephone charges will result. A maximum speed for an Internet modem is 56 kbps (kilobits per second). Each character on the keyboard is made up of a code of eight bits. This means a modem working at this speed could receive over 6000 characters in a second.

ISDN (integrated services digital network)

ISDN links share the same copper cable as an ordinary telephone but the computer data travelling along the wire is in digital form (1s and 0s). This means that there is no need for a modem to convert the signals into voice (analogue) waves. ISDN lines provide faster data transfer rates than ordinary telephone lines and transmissions are also more error-free. Typical data transfer speeds are 64 kbps in each direction. One noticeable difference in speed can be observed when connecting to the Internet; 2 to 5 seconds for ISDN rather than up to 30 seconds with a modem.

ADSL (asymmetric digital subscriber line)

ADSL, like the ISDN line, uses the existing copper telephone lines but provides even faster data speeds. From the customer (home, school or business) to the Internet service provider, data is sent at speeds of up to 640 kbps. In the other direction, from the Internet to customer, data rates can reach 8 mbps (8 million bits per second). These speeds allow full multimedia access from the Internet including 'real-time' video, for example, movies on demand. Customers with ADSL access are connected to the Internet 24 hours a day for a fixed monthly charge.

Broadband

Broadband is the name given to a data communication channel that has a wide bandwidth and can carry a large quantity of data. Under a recent government scheme, many of the schools in the UK are being connected to the Internet through broadband connections. This may vary from a dedicated 2 Mbps fibre-optic connection between the school and the Internet to shared access between a number of schools. ADSL technology is also classified as a broadband connection.

Internet

The Internet is a huge international network made up of many smaller networks linked together like a spider's web. It started as a 'self-healing' communication system for the US government in case of nuclear disaster. It was then taken up by the academic community to exchange research material. It grew to include business and personal networks and is now a vast network spanning the globe.

The Internet provides a vast range of information resources which can be accessed from your school or home computer. This information can be placed onto the Web by the millions of different users around the world without any form of regulation. This means that care must be taken when viewing different sites. Some material is very exact, detailed and informative; other sources may hold inaccurate information, and some sites hold quite offensive material.

All that is required to use the Internet is:

- a computer
- an ISDN, ADSL or modem connection and telephone line
- communications software
- access to an ISP (Internet service provider).

There are many organisations providing the link, or point of presence (PoP), where you dial in over the telephone (normally a local call) to make your connection to the Internet. These organisations, known as Internet service providers, supply the communications software and some may charge a small monthly subscription while others offer a free service. Some major ISPs include BT Internet, Freeserve, Virgin, CompuServe, Demon Internet, UK Online and AOL.

WAP mobile phones

Wireless application protocol, or WAP for short, was first introduced in 1998 and provides Internet access for mobile phones. The screens on the phones are small so cut-down versions of Internet pages without graphics are best for downloading. Current applications include banking and travel. For example, a number of hotels across the country enable WAP mobile users to check if accommodation is available, make reservations and access travel directions through the small screen.

In 2002/2003, it is forecast that the third generation of mobile phones will be available. These will enable much larger quantities of data to be received and transmitted from the phone and will allow colour Internet pages to be viewed.

Email

Email, or electronic mail, is a way of sending messages, data, files or graphics to other users on the network. Subscribers to the Internet are given an email address, eg info@pearson.co.uk. Email allows messages to be sent to anyone on the network, even on the other side of the world, for the price of a local telephone call.

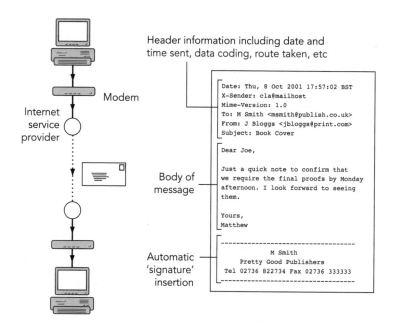

Header information including date and time sent, data coding, route taken, etc

Modem

Internet service provider

Body of message

Automatic 'signature' insertion

```
Date: Thu, 8 Oct 2001 17:57:02 BST
X-Sender: cla@mailhost
Mime-Version: 1.0
To: M Smith <msmith@publish.co.uk>
From: J Bloggs <jbloggs@print.com>
Subject: Book Cover

Dear Joe,

Just a quick note to confirm that
we require the final proofs by Monday
afternoon. I look forward to seeing
them.

Yours,
Matthew

-----------------------------------
             M Smith
       Pretty Good Publishers
  Tel 02736 822734 Fax 02736 333333
-----------------------------------
```

When a message arrives, it is directed to the inbox of the user's mailbox. If they are not online when the message arrives, it is stored for them on the server of the user's ISP or on their company's mail server. Often these messages only take minutes to travel around the world.

After reading this mail, the user can:

- delete the message
- file the message by storing it on disk
- send back a reply
- forward the message on to one or more other people.

As well as sending and receiving emails, files can be attached to the text message and passed to other users. These can be word processor documents, spreadsheets, database files or graphic images. This is a fast and efficient method of transferring data but care must be taken as virus programs are also sometimes passed with attached files and activated when the file is opened.

Spam and unsolicited mail

Spam is the name given to unsolicited emails that are sent out in large quantities to users on the Internet. Unsolicited mail is mail that has not been requested by the user. Spammers, the people that send spam emails, may send hundreds of thousands of Internet users the same message every day. One spammer in the US was reported to be sending as many as 25 million 'junk' emails every day. The contents of spam emails include 'get-rich-quick' schemes, chain mail and pyramid sales schemes, miracle health cures, loan and credit schemes and pornographic material. Spam is a nuisance as it clogs up the Internet, slowing down the network for genuine users and it takes time and money to remove spam email from mailboxes each day.

Email security

It is important to realise that email messages are not, in general, secure. It is very easy for individuals to intercept an email message in transit and examine its contents. It is also a simple matter for those with sufficient technical knowledge to forge an email from a particular person. In these respects, sending an email message is analogous to sending a postcard.

There are a number of software packages available, such as PGP (Pretty Good Privacy), which encrypt email messages before you send them, so that they cannot easily be read by anyone other than the intended recipient. Several email packages now support digital signatures, whereby an additional piece of data is added to each email message that you send which can be used to verify that an email really is from you.

Electronic bulletin boards

Electronic bulletin boards are an electronic form of a noticeboard. When users on the network visit the bulletin board site, they can read messages or leave their own for others to read. It is also possible to collect software programs from bulletin board areas. Usenet is one example of a bulletin board.

Usenet is a collection of newsgroups each on a single theme such as football, cooking or books. Each newsgroup contains postings from people, some providing information, some requesting information. When new announcements are made or queries asked, an ongoing discussion may start in the newsgroup. Nearly all Usenet newsgroups have FAQ (frequently asked questions) sections which hold answers to the most commonly asked questions. It is considered polite (or correct 'netiquette') for new users to read this information first before asking questions.

Internet chat

The chat program allows Internet users to type text messages to each other in a real-time conversation. Often Internet chat takes place in 'chat rooms' where 20 or 30 users can chat together by typing text messages. As well as typing messages for the whole room to see, individuals in the room can be selected and sent private messages. Visiting chat rooms can certainly encourage users to increase their keyboard typing speeds in order to take an active part in conversations! Many users make use of the 'net language' with abbreviations like BRB (be right back), LOL (laughing out loud) and IYSWIM (if you see what I mean). Some chat rooms for children are monitored and any antisocial behaviour or language results in these users being expelled from the room.

World Wide Web (WWW)

The World Wide Web is what draws most people onto the 'Net'. The Web allows users to publish multimedia pages, containing text, graphics, sound and video information for users of the Internet to view.

Businesses, schools and individuals can make their own Web site pages. The language used to do this is called hypertext markup language (HTML). Alternatively, there are graphical packages which will write the HTML for you. Examples of such software include Microsoft® FrontPage 2000 and Macromedia Dreamweaver.

Different Web pages can be linked using hypertext hotlinks; in other words, new pages are selected by clicking with the mouse on the linking text or graphics. Each Web page on the Internet has a unique address, starting with the letters http:// (standing for hypertext transfer protocol). These Web addresses are termed URLs (uniform resource locators). An example of a Web site address is: http://www.pearsonpublishing.co.uk/.

Web browsers

A Web browser is a piece of software for viewing the content of Web pages. It interprets the HTML and displays text and graphics on the screen accordingly. There is a common standard for how this should be done. However, different Web browsers interpret the commands slightly differently. This means that Web designers have to plan and test carefully to ensure that the end user sees what they want them to.

Extra features or interactivity can be added to Web pages using JavaScript, CGI scripts, or plug-ins such as Macromedia Flash. These can make Web sites very dynamic and exciting, but not all users will be able to see the material.

Web browsers also allow you to download material from Web sites to your hard disk – software updates, graphics, video clips, games, and much more. However, you need to obtain copyright permission to be allowed to publish or distribute any material you have downloaded.

Researching information

In order to find Web pages containing material on a specific subject, a search engine can be used. This is a Web site which, when you type in a few words or phrases, can find Web pages whose content is in some way related. It will then present these as a list of hyperlinks, usually with a short description.

The Internet can provide resource material on almost any subject but it must be used with care. There is no guarantee that information contained in an Internet article is accurate. Look for documents from official Web sites like government or company sources; they are more likely to contain accurate facts rather than other people's opinions. When searching for information by using search engines, think carefully about the key words you use, otherwise you may have thousands of article references returned.

The list below indicates some of the advantages and disadvantages of using the Internet for research material:

Advantages:

- The Internet is readily available from most computers.
- There is a huge amount of information available on most subjects.
- Articles are updated daily.
- Search engines are available to help find topics.
- Information is available in multimedia form.
- Email can be used to request further information.

Disadvantages:

- Cost of the equipment.
- There is no guarantee that the information is accurate.
- It can be difficult to find the specific information required from searches.

Questions

1   When using a computer on a local area network (LAN):

   a   why is it necessary to have a password?

   ....

   b   why should passwords be changed regularly?

   ....

   c   why, when a user changes their password, are they asked to type in the new password, and then type it in again?

   ....

2 Complete the following sentences by choosing the correct words from the list below:

> WAN   modem   OCR   email   word processor   MAN   byte
> model   formatting   printer   LAN   virus

"A .... connects the computers in a school. Students can also access the school's computers from home using a .... The school has access to the Internet which is a .... , and students can send messages using ...."

3 The diagram below shows the layout of a network used in a veterinary practice. A workstation and printer is located in every consulting room.

a What type of network topology (structure) is used in this LAN?

....

b Give two advantages of having a network instead of stand-alone machines in each consulting room.

....

....

It is decided to join all the veterinary practices in the county to form a wide area network (WAN).

c What extra device would be needed to join the LAN to a WAN?

....

d What is the function of this device?

....

e What security problems might arise for the practice by linking up to the WAN? (See *Chapter 18*, page 107.)

....

....

13 Video conferencing

The term video conferencing refers to users communicating across networks using audio and video images. The fact that schools and home users are now able to use video conferencing on their PCs is due to the rapid advances in computer technology. A camera, often placed on the top of the monitor, records the digital images of the user while a microphone captures the speech. These signals are then transmitted across the network to the receiving station where the image is displayed in a window on the monitor. In addition to the audio and video signals, data from applications can also be transmitted. For example, if a user is demonstrating using graphs from data in a spreadsheet, then this could also be transmitted.

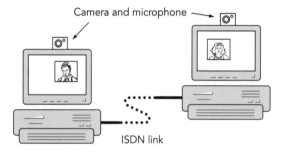

Camera and microphone

ISDN link

A simple video conferencing set-up

Video images generate large quantities of data and so it is necessary to compress the data and transmit it across high-speed channels. One method of compressing data is by using a codec card in the PC. The codec hardware **co**mpresses the data leaving the computer and **dec**ompresses the data arriving at the computer. The speed of data transmission across telephone lines using modems is not really fast enough for effective transmission. It is necessary to use ISDN lines (see page 81) that provide transmission speeds at 64 kbps (kilobits per second), or faster services like ADSL and broadband connections.

The video image at the receiving station is displayed in a window. There are two commonly agreed standards for the size of these windows. One is approximately one-fifth the size of an SVGA screen where the image is refreshed between 15 and 25 times a second. The second size is smaller, approximately $1/20$ of the screen area but, as less data is being transmitted, the refresh rate is up to 30 times a second.

Video conferencing installations

Depending on the number of people involved at each end of the video conferencing link, the arrangement of cameras and the size of the display screen will vary. Conferencing systems can be broadly divided into three groups as follows:

- **Desktop systems** – These are the simplest and least expensive systems to set up. The computer requires a fixed focus camera, microphone, speakers, PC card and ISDN line or LAN (local area network) link. Desktop systems are designed for single users.

- **Mobile units** – These video conferencing systems are installed on trolleys using larger display monitors more suited to use with small groups (eg up to ten users). The cameras are generally more sophisticated with additional pan, tilt and zoom functions. Mobile units are ideal for moving between classrooms in schools.

- **Room installations** – Equipping a room with video conferencing facilities to handle larger groups (eg 30 users) requires more sophisticated and expensive equipment. Several microphones will be necessary in the room and the camera needs to be voice-activated or manually controlled by a 'director' to point to the speaker. Large display units or projection systems are used to show the video and data being transmitted.

Benefits of video conferencing

There are various benefits to using video conferencing. For example, in schools, students taking Modern Foreign Language courses can interact directly with other schools in different countries. Students can use the global Internet links to experience different cultures. Junior school pupils can find out more about school life at a secondary school by linking with older students at local schools to discuss topics in the different curriculum subjects. Older students can gain valuable knowledge from career sites and links with colleges and universities.

In business, video conferencing is ideal for meetings between remote sites. Companies often have offices in different countries around the world and traditional meetings take time to organise and involve considerable time and expense in the travelling and accommodation.

14 Flow charts

Flow charts are used to illustrate processes and operations in computers. Using a flow chart diagram in your coursework report can be valuable in outlining the way your program works. There are a number of different types of flow chart. This book looks at two sorts: program flow charts and data flow diagrams.

Program flow charts

These are used to show the operations involved in a computer program. Different symbols are used to represent particular operations. Flow charts can be constructed before the program instructions are written to help the programmer, or they can be constructed afterwards to help document the program. Documentation is important to help other users understand how the program works so that future maintenance can take place.

Symbol	Description	Example
◯	**Connector** Used when a flow chart continues on the next page	(A) bottom of first page / (A) top of second page
⬭	**Terminator** Used for 'start' and 'stop'	STOP
▱	**Input/output** Used to show input and output of data	Read name
◇	**Decision** Used to illustrate different paths being taken based on decisions. Decision boxes can have more than two exits	Is N>10? No / Yes
▭	**Process** Used to represent a sequence of instructions or operations not involving a decision	Initialise variables
▯	**Subroutine** Used to indicate a sequence of instructions which will have its own flow chart elsewhere	Validate check digit

Example of a program flow chart

The following flow chart illustrates graphically the sequence of control instructions required to open a security door. A numeric keypad with a pass code of '1324' will unlock the door, but if more than three wrong codes are entered, an alarm will be triggered.

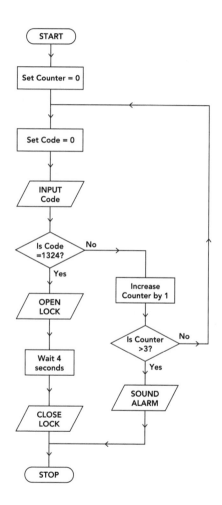

Data flow diagrams (DFDs)

These diagrams show how a procedure or operation takes place with reference to the flow of data. This is often a useful illustration to include in GCSE coursework projects to show the way data is processed.

Symbol	Description	Example
	Data source or destination Usually people or departments that supply or receive data	Customer
	Process An operation that is performed on the data, eg calculations, sorting or printing	Print customer details
	Data store Represents any storage: disk, magnetic tape, paper, filing cabinets, etc	Master file
→	**Data flow** Shows the movement of data. The arrows should always be labelled	→ Members' details, name and address

Example of a data flow diagram

A customer sends off an order to a mail order company for goods. The company checks the order and payment when it arrives and then passes the order for processing. A 'picking list' is printed for the warehouse where the goods are packed and despatched to the customer. Details of the order are recorded in a 'customer's file' and an invoice is despatched. The stock levels in the stock file are adjusted as the order is being processed.

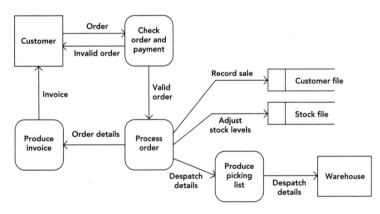

15 System design and development

GCSE ICT projects and coursework

When we set out to use Information and Communication Technology to assist with a particular task we follow a structured series of processes. The stages in this series are similar whether carried out by a team of programmers for a company or a student doing a coursework project for their ICT GCSE. The general pattern for the stages is as follows:

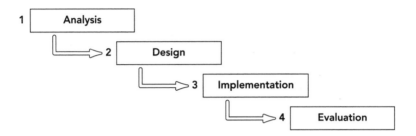

These two additional parts must also be included, either as separate stages, or as part of the ones above:

For GCSE coursework you are required to investigate how ICT could assist in a task or process. Remember, when you come to write up your coursework project to include sketches and diagrams, tables, graphs, flow charts and photographs to help to explain your project. Before you can show that an ICT solution would be beneficial, it is necessary to understand the current process in detail. This can be done in one or more ways as outlined below.

Examining the task:

- interview the person(s) currently doing the task
- ask the person(s) doing the task to complete a questionnaire
- observe the way the task is currently being done and make notes
- collect and study the data, forms, screen displays, printouts currently in use.

Feasibility study

After a detailed examination of the problem, it is necessary to look at whether a computerised solution is the right approach. Will the computerised solution being proposed reduce paperwork, speed up the processing, give better stock control, create fewer mistakes, provide better reports for the managers? Will these potential benefits outweigh the costs involved of introducing the new system? It should be clear that the answer to this question is 'Yes' before a decision to proceed is reached.

Top-down design

There are several methods of designing a solution for a chosen problem but one of the most popular methods is using a 'top-down design' approach. Starting with the main task, this is broken down into sub-tasks. These sub-tasks are then further divided to show more detail.

An example of a top-down approach is shown in the illustration below. Here a computer program is being designed for teachers that will enable them to write reports for students:

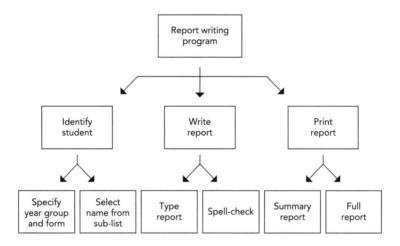

The bottom layer would then be subdivided further until the whole task comprised a set of simple tasks.

Testing

Testing is a very important part in the development of an ICT system, whether in business or in school coursework. A plan for testing and the results of testing should also be documented to show that it has been carried out in a logical fashion. To test a program, data needs to be used.

For some programs, a data capture form can be designed to record the data before it is entered into the computer. Data capture forms should be designed carefully so that they match the input screen and make the data entry easier and less prone to errors (see page 52).

What data should be used?

- Normal data that is expected by the program. The processing of this data can be compared to the original methods used to ensure that the program is processing the data correctly.

- Data with known errors and extremes of data (eg very large and small numbers) can be entered to see how the program copes. This is where the validation of data is important (see page 53).

- Large quantities of data can be entered to see if the program fails or if its processing speed slows down too much.

- All the functions and features built into the program need to be tested in a methodical manner.

Documentation

There are two types of documentation – user documentation and technical documentation:

- **User documentation** – The user documentation is designed for the person using the new system and should include:
  - how to load and run the program
  - how to use the different features of the program such as entering data, saving, editing, sorting and printing
  - a troubleshooting section to deal with exceptional circumstances where things do not work as they should.

  User documentation should be written in plain English without any technical words or terms.

- **Technical documentation** – This documentation contains the technical details of the program together with structure diagrams to assist other programmers and systems analysts. It is, therefore, written using technical words and terms. Technical documentation allows changes to be made to the program in future years when the original developers may no longer be around. Programs may need to be improved or updated. For example, many programs were altered to cater for the date change in the year 2000.

Checklist

Below are some guidance notes showing what may be included at each of the four stages of the project. Documentation and testing have been included as parts of the main four stages:

Analysis

- [ ] Identify a task which will make sensible use of the ICT tools
- [ ] Gather information about the task, eg show how it is currently done without the aid of a computer
- [ ] Define the problem
- [ ] Who are the potential users? Gather their views. Use a questionnaire or interview
- [ ] Produce a design specification to include all aspects of the task – include resource requirements
- [ ] Show the flow of data through the system with a data flow diagram
- [ ] What are the limitations of the potential users? Would they be able to manage your proposed system?
- [ ] What are the limitations imposed by the resources available – equipment, software packages and peripherals?
- [ ] Outline the objectives for the project
- [ ] Specify the data sources required for the task
- [ ] Other:

Design

- [ ] Look at a range of different solutions using different methods and software packages
- [ ] Consider the computer versus the non-computer solution and the effect of resources on the chosen design
- [ ] Choose one solution and justify the choice
- [ ] Show with system flow charts, data flow diagrams and block diagrams how the proposed solution will operate
- [ ] Ensure that the chosen design proposal matches the requirements of the potential users

- ☐ Describe the structure and quantity of input data required and the output from the system
- ☐ Show the design of forms, reports and queries that might be used in the system
- ☐ Explain if validation and verification of data are required/used in the solution
- ☐ Design a comprehensive test strategy for the system
- ☐ Other:

Implementation

- ☐ Show the use of the software packages and document some of the features used
- ☐ State how the solution works and use diagrams to illustrate this
- ☐ Ensure the results you produce match the design section
- ☐ Produce documentation for the user giving instructions on using the program, resource requirements and a troubleshooting guide
- ☐ Test your solution following the test strategy stated in the design section, and produce the evidence of testing
- ☐ Other:

Evaluation

- ☐ Compare the final solution with the design objectives set out in the analysis section
- ☐ Test results from your solution may be given here or in the implementation section
- ☐ Have your solution tested *in situ* doing the real task as set out in the analysis
- ☐ Document the opinions of other users testing and using your solution
- ☐ State the improvements made to the program as a result of testing
- ☐ State any enhancements and improvements that could be implemented
- ☐ Other:

16 Applications of ICT

Computers are now used in almost every aspect of daily life. The examples that follow show a range of uses and illustrate some of the input, output and processing functions involved.

Computers in shops

It is important for shops to know how much stock to hold. Too much stock will take up valuable space, is costly and the shop runs the risk of products not being sold before their 'sell-by' date. Too little stock and customers will be unhappy when they cannot buy what they need. In larger stores and supermarkets, the control of stock by constantly monitoring the sales is done by EPOS (electronic point of sale) terminals, ie the checkout.

Bar codes

Each product has a bar code which represents the product's number. When the product is purchased, the scanner reads the black and white lines of the bar code to identify the product. The bar code number is passed to the computer which holds details of all the products in a large datafile. An itemised receipt for the customer is produced, and the records are adjusted in the stock file.

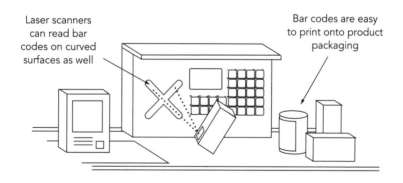

Bar codes being laser scanned at a checkout till

The advantages of using an EPOS system for the customer include:

- much faster service at the checkout till – without a scanner, the number on each item would need to be keyed in by the shop assistant
- scanning the goods gives greater accuracy than keying product numbers
- an itemised receipt describes the purchase and shows the price
- the computerised system makes multibuys easy to operate, eg 'Buy two, get a third free'
- goods are more likely to be fresh as the system improves stock control.

The advantages of using an EPOS system for the store manager include:

- customers pass through the checkouts more quickly and with fewer errors being made by the assistants
- goods in the shop do not have to be individually priced: only the edge of shelf price label needs to match the price in the computer
- the control of stock is fully automated: as each product passes through the checkout, the level of stock is adjusted
- more efficient stock control means less stock needs to be kept, thus saving on both space and money
- as all the sales are monitored, the managers can monitor the demand at the checkouts and ensure the correct staffing level.

Stock control

The manager of the store determines the minimum amount of stock for each product in the store. For example, this might be 200 cans of peas. As each tin of peas is purchased, the number in stock is reduced by 1. When the number in stock falls below the minimum stock level (in this case 200), a message to reorder more cans is sent by the computer to the head office where all the orders are collated and dispatched to the suppliers.

Recent developments

The large supermarket chains are constantly striving to improve their services to customers ahead of their competitors. New ideas based on Information and Communication Technology include:

- allowing customers to scan the product bar codes themselves
- home shopping where the order is sent via the Internet to the local store where the goods are selected and packed.

Computers in banks and building societies

Banks were one of the first organisations to use computers. Introduced in the 1950s, computers were well established by the mid-1960s for tasks like processing cheques, calculating interest and keeping customers' accounts.

Processing cheques

Each day in Britain, millions of cheques are cashed. Without computers, this would not be possible and the financial world would grind to a halt. The key to processing so much data lies in the coded characters at the bottom of the cheque which are printed using an ink containing magnetic particles.

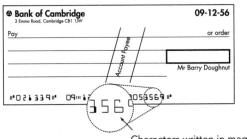

Characters written in magnetic ink

When new (unused) cheques are sent to customers, three sets of numbers are already printed onto each cheque using the magnetic ink. When the cheque is used, and in due course presented to the bank, a fourth number, the amount the cheque has been made out for, is typed on using the special ink. The four sets of numbers – the bank's sort code, the customer's account number, the individual cheque number and the amount – provide all the information needed to process the cheque automatically.

Using a recording head similar to that on a tape recorder, the numbers can be read into the computer at great speed (3000 cheques per minute). This input process is called MICR (magnetic ink character recognition – see page 9).

ATMs (automatic teller machines)

Obtaining cash at any time of the day or night from a cash dispenser (the ATM) is often more convenient than visiting the bank or building society. Also, employers have moved away from paying their workers in cash. Instead, they transfer funds directly through to the workers' accounts so the need for these cash dispensers has grown.

To obtain cash from the machine:

1 insert the card into the slot

2 enter the PIN (personal identification number)

3 choose the service required (cash, check balance, request statement, etc)

4 select the amount of cash required

5 take back the card

6 take the money

7 take the receipt (if requested).

(When these machines were first installed, points 5 and 6 in the procedure above were reversed. This led to people forgetting to take their cards.)

Plastic cards

The card used to withdraw cash is a plastic card with a magnetic stripe (similar to Access, Visa and MasterCard). The magnetic stripe holds about 72 characters and is coded with data related to the customer's account.

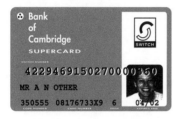
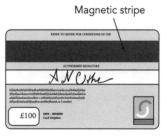

Magnetic stripe

Electronic funds transfer (EFT)

When a cash dispenser is used, the amount of money withdrawn is removed from the user's account. This movement of money electronically is referred to as an electronic funds transfer. When paying for shopping in a supermarket using 'plastic' such as a Switch card, the payment is transferred electronically from the customer's account to the shop's account. The computerised till is known as a point of sale (POS) terminal. This transfer of funds is therefore called EFTPOS (electronic funds transfer point of sale).

Computers in manufacturing

The car manufacturing industry was one of the first to use computer-controlled robots in the construction of vehicles. Since that time, their use has become widespread across all sections of manufacturing. In order to increase productivity and decrease costs, manufacturers have found it necessary to replace workers with machines.

Although the initial cost of installing these computer-controlled machines is high, the low running costs quickly pay for the investment by decreasing labour costs.

The advantages include:

- continuous operation, 24 hours per day, without tiring or tea breaks
- faster operations: a robotic arm can average one weld per second
- consistent and accurate work
- the ability to handle heavy loads
- the ability to work in hostile environments.

The diagram below illustrates some of the benefits:

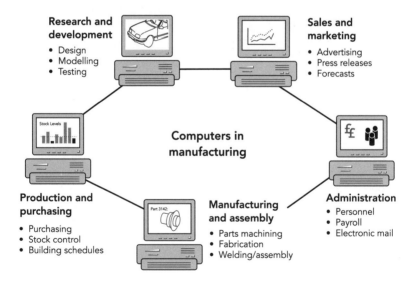

Research and development
- Design
- Modelling
- Testing

Sales and marketing
- Advertising
- Press releases
- Forecasts

Computers in manufacturing

Production and purchasing
- Purchasing
- Stock control
- Building schedules

Manufacturing and assembly
- Parts machining
- Fabrication
- Welding/assembly

Administration
- Personnel
- Payroll
- Electronic mail

Computers in other applications

Police Force: The Police National Computer (PNC) consists of several mainframe computers holding important files which help the police force in their investigation work. There are datafiles for cars containing information on the registration number, make, model and colour, and the owner's details. There are datafiles for suspects, criminals, and wanted and missing persons. There are files holding fingerprint and DNA data that allow police officers to search and match evidence at the scene of a crime with possible suspects.

Hospitals: The patients' records in a hospital are often kept on computer files. This allows data to be retrieved rapidly and transmitted electronically to different hospitals or surgeries. As patients' dates of birth are held on file, it is a straightforward procedure to use the mailmerge facility of the computer software to send out reminder letters for inoculations. Computer equipment is used in intensive care wards to monitor patients, with heartbeat, temperature, pressure, and movement sensors inputting critical data from the patient. Databases are held with details of patients requiring transplant surgery. In the event of transplant organs becoming available, these can be matched quickly to an appropriate patient.

Questions

1 Two benefits to shop managers of using point of sale machines at supermarket checkouts are:

   a   managers can locate customers in the store at any time

   b   customers pass through the checkouts more quickly and with fewer errors being made

   c   it is easier to put the shopping into bags

   d   an itemised receipt describes the purchase and shows the price

   e   stock levels are adjusted automatically as the goods are scanned at the checkout.

2 There are only three sets of magnetic ink numbers on a bank cheque before it has been used. What do these numbers represent?

   a   ....

   b   ....

   c   ....

17 Effects of ICT on society

As young people at school you are used to having computers around. You may have a computer at home to play games on or to help you with your school work. You will certainly use computers in your lessons at school. If you look around, you will see computers used in shops or your parents' workplaces, and you will often hear computers talked about on television.

Growth of computing

If you have a chance to visit the computing section at the Science Museum, you will see how very recent the development of computers has been. Engines, cars and motorcycles were invented over a hundred years ago, and in comparison to computer development they have changed very little.

The first electronic computers, using glass tubes called valves, were constructed around 50 years ago. These first computers were used to calculate firing tables for field guns and to crack German codes during the war. Their processing power was very small by today's standards and the machines filled large rooms and consumed enormous quantities of power. The widespread use of computers in homes, schools and businesses only began about 20 years ago. Even today, this growth continues; month by month, computers become more sophisticated, have larger memories, better displays, faster processing, new features and yet their price remains the same or even falls.

Effect on society

This new age of computers is having an enormous impact on our lives. Some people wish it had never happened and long for the 'good old days', before computers, when the pace of life was much slower and less complicated. Others are greatly attracted by the opportunities this new technology offers. Life as we know it today, however, could not exist if this modern technology were removed. Without the aid of computerised technology, we could not handle all the cheques written every day and the millions of telephone calls made. Even if all the unemployed people in the country were brought in to assist, it would not be possible. Our standard of living would fall, prices would rise and on an international scale, any country that adopted this approach would be bound to fail in the competitive world in which we live.

Communication around the world has become almost instantaneous. For the price of a local telephone call, one can send messages around the globe by email. Huge quantities of information are available through the Internet and new skills are required to select and filter information needed from the various sources and articles. Information and Communication Technology allows documents to be faxed from one side of the world to the other. ICT is also responsible for the advances in digital communication, satellite and cable television.

Communication through email and the access to information through the Internet is having a dramatic impact on our lives. Many more people are now working from home and this is set to increase as cameras mounted above monitors allow visual contact with other users. One possibility for future development is that all computers will have a radio link to the Internet, using similar technology to mobile phones.

It was once said that the use of computers would lead to the paperless office. In fact, computers generate far more paper than we had before. The amount of computerised mail that is delivered to our houses (bills, forms, advertising leaflets) shows that there is a lot of information about people held on computer files. Some data held on computers is highly confidential, for example, medical, financial and criminal data, and some of this data will be incorrect due to errors in the data sourcing and entry. These are issues that may affect our lives.

Effect on jobs

The introduction of computers has resulted in the loss of many jobs. In the early days, many of the jobs lost were those of unskilled workers whose repetitive tasks were replaced by machines. More recently, computerisation has replaced jobs across most sections of the workplace. Even middle managers who make complex decisions using well-structured procedures have found that computer programs can replace them at a lower cost to the company.

The majority of jobs have been lost from the manufacturing industries but there has been an increase in jobs in the service sector; shops, hotels, catering and leisure industries. Part of this is due to the increased wealth generated by the more technologically advanced industries. Many new jobs have been created in the ICT and computing area, both in the manufacturing and service industries.

If a manufacturing plant invests in computerised equipment to replace its workers, then it will become more competitive as productivity rises and labour costs are reduced. However, some of its workers may be made redundant. If it does not computerise, the high labour costs and lower productivity result in the goods becoming less competitive and so the company starts to fail and all the workers lose their jobs. In addition, the nation loses the ability to manufacture those goods at a standard comparable to other countries. This illustrates the dilemma faced by employers, trade unions and governments.

Many people have had to retrain in new areas of work as computerised systems have replaced their original jobs. It is necessary in society today to have a flexible workforce where individuals may have to retrain for employment two or three times during their working lives. It is also important for individuals to understand how computers work and the effects that Information and Communication Technology has on their lives so that they can influence the changes that are taking place and ensure that a better quality of life results from those changes.

Questions

1   Information and Communication Technology makes it easier for people to work from home. Describe one advantage and one disadvantage of home working.

....

....

....

....

....

....

2   Describe how the increased use of ICT for home shopping and banking may cause changes in society.

....

....

....

....

....

....

....

18 Data protection

The Data Protection Act, 1998

The 'right to privacy' is a right we all expect. We do not expect personal details such as our age, medical records, personal family details, political and religious beliefs to be freely available to everybody. With the growth of Information and Communication Technology, large databases are able to hold huge quantities of information and global networks are able to share and distribute this information around the world in seconds. In order to control this development and to protect people's right to privacy, the Data Protection Act was introduced. The first Act became law in 1984 but was replaced by the 1998 Act that also incorporates the European Commission Directive.

If any person, organisation, company or business wishes to hold personal information about people, they must register with the Office of the Data Protection Commissioner.

The Data Protection Act contains eight basic principles. A summary of these is shown below:

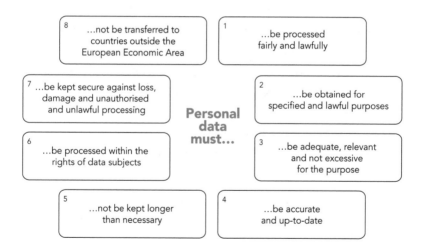

8 ...not be transferred to countries outside the European Economic Area

1 ...be processed fairly and lawfully

7 ...be kept secure against loss, damage and unauthorised and unlawful processing

Personal data must...

2 ...be obtained for specified and lawful purposes

6 ...be processed within the rights of data subjects

3 ...be adequate, relevant and not excessive for the purpose

5 ...not be kept longer than necessary

4 ...be accurate and up-to-date

Note: The first of the eight principles listed above contains the most details in the Act as different conditions apply according to the nature of the data held. Also, unlike the 1984 Act, manual records containing data are now subject to legislation.

Personal data

What is actually meant by personal data? It is data that can identify a living person and allow an opinion to be expressed about that person. For example, just a name and address is not considered personal data. However, if the data also includes their date of birth and earnings, then this is personal data as the data allows opinions to be expressed about the person. The data can be further classified as 'sensitive' personal data. This includes details of:

- racial or ethnic origins
- political opinions
- religious beliefs
- whether members of trade unions
- their physical or mental health or condition
- sexual life.

Rights of data subjects

In the sixth of the eight principles shown, the rights of the data subject were mentioned. The rights of individuals have increased substantially in the 1998 Act. The following offers a summary.

The individual can:

- be given a copy of the data held
- prevent processing of the data if it is likely to cause damage or distress
- prevent the data being used for direct marketing
- prevent automated decisions being made on the basis of data held
- receive compensation for damage and distress caused by use of the data
- have data corrected, blocked and erased if inaccurate
- make a request to the Data Protection Commissioner if they feel the Act has been contravened.

Exemptions

There are certain exemptions to the Act and the rules governing the need to register data. A summary of the main exemptions to the Act include data that is:

- related to national security
- associated with crime and taxation
- involved in health, education and social work

- used in regulatory activities by public 'watch dogs'
- processed for special (journalistic, literary and artistic) purposes
- used in research, history and statistics
- required by law and in connection with legal proceedings being disclosed
- held for domestic purposes, eg household, personal and family affairs.

Looking after computer data

In business, the data stored in a computer can be hundreds of times more valuable than the actual computer equipment. This data may include all the company's financial records, all its customers' details, records of the stock held, etc. Losing this data could, in some cases, put companies out of business.

Data can be damaged or destroyed in the following ways:

- breakdown of hardware, particularly disk drives
- mistakes by office staff, eg deleting files
- poor office practice, eg not taking a regular back-up of datafiles and not checking for viruses
- hackers gaining access to systems and changing/deleting data
- computer fraud where data is changed to benefit individuals
- theft of computer equipment
- fire, floods, hurricanes, earthquakes, etc, destroying equipment
- infection of systems and data by computer viruses
- deliberate and malicious damage by staff.

Back-ups

Taking a back-up of the data from the hard disk drive of a computer or from the hard disk of a server running a network is vital. One certain fact is that a hard disk drive will not run forever. If a back-up is taken at the end of each day, then the most that can be lost is one day's work. Often special tape streamer units are used which saves the data onto magnetic tape cassettes. These cassette tapes can typically hold up to 26 GB of data allowing all the data on the server's hard drives to be backed up. A number of tapes should be used in rotation so that a back-up copy can always be kept away from the premises.

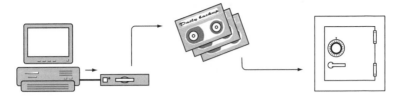

Data is backed up onto tape and then put in a safe place

These tape back-ups should be kept away from the original data, in another building or on another site. Businesses may encourage office staff to take back-up tapes home with them so that data will not be lost through theft from the offices. Tapes kept on-site should be deposited safely each evening in a fireproof safe.

Hackers

A hacker is a person who breaks codes and passwords to gain unauthorised entry to computer systems. Some hackers can do an enormous amount of damage if they break into a computer system. For some people, the challenge of breaking the codes is irresistible and so precautions have to be taken. Stand-alone computers are usually safe as there is no connection for the hackers to break into. Computers which form part of networks or those with external links, such as attached modems, are in danger from hackers. It is necessary to use passwords to log on to the computer system and it is important to change these passwords at regular intervals.

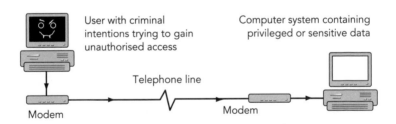

Computers connected to networks or modems are at risk from hacking

Not all hackers cause harm, ethical hackers help to highlight gaps in security and alert organisations to possible security risks.

Computer fraud

Computer fraud is a criminal activity where computer operators use the computer to their own advantage. It is thought that only one in ten cases of computer fraud are reported. There are a number of reasons for this:

- it is very hard to track down and the people committing the crime are often very clever
- offenders are often young, with no previous criminal records
- when fraud is discovered in a company, it is often not publicised as news of the fraud may damage the image of the company.

One example of computer fraud involved a computer operator who found a blank payroll form. He completed the form, making up the details for an imaginary person working in the company. Each month, as the pay cheques were produced from the company computer, he was able to slip the cheque into his pocket without anyone realising.

Computer viruses

In the same way that human viruses use the human body's own system to reproduce themselves, so computer viruses are small programs that 'hijack' a computer and use it to reproduce and spread themselves.

How viruses spread

There are thousands of different viruses and more are being created every month by people intent on damaging other people's computer systems. The viruses attach themselves to computer programs and datafiles. They then spread by copying themselves onto floppy disks, then onto other hard disks and also across networks – all without the knowledge of the user. It is quite possible to connect to the Internet, download an email message and gain a virus in the process.

How they are activated

Viruses are activated in different ways. Some are activated by the internal clock and will start running on a particular day, eg Friday 13th. Others activate when a series of conditions are true, eg when a certain combination of keys are pressed on the keyboard. Virus programs generally destroy and corrupt data on the computer's hard disk.

Removing viruses

There are a number of anti-virus programs available for wiping out viruses but, with any anti-virus program, it is important to have regular updates to deal with new viruses. When the anti-virus software is run, it scans the hard disk looking for virus patterns. This software cleans the virus off the disk and alerts the user to the damage caused by the virus.

The Computer Misuse Act, 1990

Hacking, computer fraud and computer viruses are all relatively new crimes that established English laws were not designed to deal with. For example, under existing laws, a hacker could only be prosecuted for the theft of electricity. To deal with these new crimes, a law was introduced in 1990 called The Computer Misuse Act. Under this law, the following offences could be dealt with:

- Hacking – unauthorised access to any program or data held in a computer. Penalty is a maximum fine of £2000 and a six month prison sentence.

- Computer fraud and blackmail. Penalty is an unlimited fine and a maximum five-year prison sentence.

- Viruses – unauthorised modification of the contents of a computer, impairing the operation of any program or reliability of data. Penalty is an unlimited fine and a maximum five-year prison sentence.

The Copyright, Designs and Patents Act, 1989

Copying computer software, or software piracy, is now a criminal offence under this 1989 Act. The Act covers stealing software, using illegally copied software and manuals, and running purchased software on two or more machines at the same time without a suitable licence. Quite often, organisations will purchase software licences to cover the number of workstations on their network. They then neglect to purchase additional software licences as they buy more workstations.

The legal penalties for breaking the copyright law include unlimited fines and up to two years in prison.

It has been estimated that half the software used is copied illegally and in some countries pirated software accounts for 90% of the total. Two organisations fight to stop software being copied:

- FAST (Federation Against Software Theft), founded in 1984, is a non-profit organisation to promote the legal use of software.

- BSA (Business Software Alliance) exist to make organisations and their employees aware of the law and encourage its implementation.

Health and safety

It is important to realise that working with computers, particularly for long periods of time, can be dangerous to your health. To create a safe working environment, the following factors should be considered.

Room and furniture design

The safest environment is a tidy and well-organised room. Electrical cables should not trail across the floor, and food and drinks should be kept well away from the computer and keyboard. Computers should be positioned so that sunlight from the window does not reflect on the screen. Sitting at the computer for long periods of time is never comfortable. Leaning back in the chair reduces the pressure on the spine but then the arms have to reach forward to the keyboard creating muscle tension which leads to aches and pains in the neck, shoulders, back and arms. Sitting upright with the feet flat, the upper arms straight down parallel with the body, and the lower arms horizontal resting on the keyboard is the best posture. Adjustable chairs that give the maximum support for the back are also best. The illustration below shows the correct position for working at a computer:

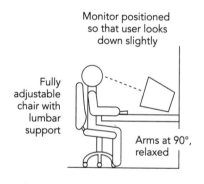

A healthy working position

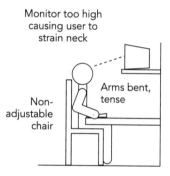

A poor working position

Even with a comfortable working environment, it is still good to stand up, stretch, move and look out of the window to relieve the eyes every 15 minutes when working at the computer.

Electrical considerations

Computers are generally connected to 240v mains electricity and must be treated with care. The computer should be properly earthed and the plugs should have the correct fuses. If the computer is moved or opened, the power cable should be the first to be disconnected and the last to be reconnected. In case of a fire, the fire extinguishers should be powder-based or CO_2 (carbon dioxide) devices. Water-based fire extinguishers should not be used on electrical appliances.

Keyboard

The standard keyboard, known as the QWERTY keyboard because of the arrangement of letters along the top row, is not a logical layout. The keyboard design is over 100 years old and was designed to reduce the typing speed so that the letters on the mechanical typewriters did not jam. The layout is now so well established that it is difficult to change but it has led to serious health problems for some typists. These workers suffer from neck, arm and hand pains called RSI (repetitive strain injury) or, as it is becoming more commonly known, WRULD (work-related upper limb disorders). Ergonomically-designed keyboards, where the keys are split and contoured for the hands, can be purchased with prices ranging from £40 to £400.

Monitor

Staring at the computer monitor for long periods can lead to eye strain and headaches. Large monitors with high resolutions are easier on the eyes. All new monitors must comply with EU standards which ensure that radiation emission is as low as possible. In 1992, the Health and Safety (Display Screen Equipment) Regulations came into force. This legislation requires that employers check that the workstation and the working environment is safe and if employees spend a significant time at the workstation, the employer must pay for eye tests.

Questions

1 Two of the statements shown below are a summary of the eight principles set out in the Data Protection Act 1998. Which two are they?

a ☐ Personal data may not be made available to the individual concerned and provision need not be made for correction.

b ☐ Data must not be kept longer than necessary.

c ☐ Those organisations that are exempt from the Data Protection Act do not need to register with the Data Protection Registrar's office but they are required by law to follow the principles of the Act.

d ☐ Data must be accurate and up-to-date.

2 Gaining access to computers illegally can cause serious problems. Describe two problems it can cause and two ways of preventing it from happening.

....

....

....

3 Explain the term computer virus, and give two precautions which should be taken to avoid a computer virus affecting a computer.

....

....

....

4 Describe two different situations when it might be necessary to use the back-up copies taken from a hard disk drive.

....

....

5 Which of the following is not exempt from the Data Protection Act? Data held:

a ☐ for national security

b ☐ to prevent crime

c ☐ by a company for direct mail

d ☐ for tax purposes.

Answers

Input devices (page 14)

1　CD-ROM – used as source of clip art pictures;
　　Scanner – to input photographs
2　Country of manufacture
3　The price of the product may need to change
4　a　Thermistor (temperature sensor) or light-
　　　　dependent resistor (light sensor)
　　b　Concept keyboard
　　c　Optical character recognition
　　d　Optical mark recognition
　　e　Magnetic stripe on a debit/credit card

Output devices (page 21)

1　Input – push button switches
　　Output – LCD display
2　Monitor, plotter
3　a　Laser printer
　　b　Ink-jet
　　c　Dot-matrix
4　a　For blind users
　　b　Flat-bed plotters, robotic arms
　　c　Digital watches, calculators

Computer memory (page 23)

　　Words in correct order are: megabytes, RAM,
　　memory, eight

Data storage (page 27)

1　Less possibility of damaging or corrupting
　　programs and data, stores much more data,
　　better graphics and sound, CD used when
　　playing the game so no need to use up
　　valuable hard disk drive space
2　To transfer programs and data between
　　computers, to keep back-ups of data, to store
　　programs and data in a safe location

Operating systems (page 30)

1　Words in correct order are: multi-processor,
　　multi-user/multi-tasking, real-time, batch
2　d　Printing a telephone directory

Human–computer interface (page 32)

1　a　The movement of the mouse to control the
　　　　screen pointer, mouse buttons to select,
　　　　drag and activate menu options
　　b　Use of drop-down menus, selection of
　　　　menu choice by clicking mouse buttons, use
　　　　of icons, dragging over text to highlight, etc

2　Another action is required first, eg you cannot
　　choose 'Edit ... paste' until a picture or text
　　has been selected and 'Edit ... copy or cut'
　　has occurred

Databases (page 56)

1　a and b
2　Words in correct order are: customer, file,
　　fields, unique, key
3　a　GEO2FLO
　　b　ART1EMC
　　c　Easier and quicker to enter, less typing
　　　　required, less likely to make spelling
　　　　mistakes, uses less computer memory
4　Range check, >0 and <13

Spreadsheets (page 61)

a　=SUM(D3:D6) or =D3+D4+D5+D6
b　i　Text (cells in row 1 or column A or C8)
　　ii　Numbers (cells B3-B6 or C3-C6)
c　Alter values in column C until required total
　　value reached
d　Words in correct order are: formatted, formula,
　　copied, D5, D8

CAD/CAM (page 65)

1　Computer aided design
2　Zooming, rotation, enlargement, boxes, circles,
　　infill, shading, colours, save, load, plot, text,
　　dimensions, scaling
3　Bigger screen (typically 20 inches+), much
　　higher resolution, more expensive

Data logging (page 71)

a　Light-dependent resistor (LDR)
b　Analogue
c　Digital
d　The substances are likely to react too quickly for
　　measurements to be taken by hand, data
　　logging equipment takes measurements with
　　high speed and accuracy
e　The light sensor would be replaced by a
　　thermistor input device positioned in the
　　liquid. The light would be removed as this
　　would act as an additional heat source

Computer control (page 76)

a　Total_cars = cars_start + cars_in – cars_out
b　If total_cars<max_cars
c　Use a pressure sensor which will respond to
　　the weight of a car but not people

Communication (pages 86 and 87)

1. a This will stop unauthorised users from logging onto the network or accessing files in another user's directory
   b A password may be seen by another user so their data will no longer be secure
   c The password is being verified to ensure that a wrong key was not pressed when the new password was typed in
2. Words in correct order are: LAN, modem, WAN, email
3. a Star topology
   b The vets can access their datafiles from any of the consulting rooms, programs can be shared, easier to back up the data (just the server to back up, not every machine)
   c Modem
   d Converts the digital signals from the computer to sound signals (analogue) so data can be sent along telephone lines
   e Unauthorised users may hack into the computer using the telephone lines and modem. They could corrupt data, introduce viruses and gain access to confidential data

Applications of ICT (page 103)

1. b and e
2. a Cheque number
   b Bank sort code
   c Account number

Effects of ICT on society (page 106)

1. Advantages: Flexible working hours, time and money not spent commuting to work, reduced costs for expensive office space, more comfortable working environment
   Disadvantages: Less interaction with colleagues generating new ideas, possible feeling of isolation, expensive telephone bills through communicating with others
2. Less interaction between people, fewer staff needed in shops and less traffic on the roads, reduced need to locate shops in expensive town and city centres, potential increase in crime using ICT

Data protection (pages 114 and 115)

1. b and d
2. Problems caused: The data may be confidential, it could be passed to business competitors, data could be changed
   Preventing: Restrict access to the computer, ensure supervisor monitors computer use, use passwords, message should be relayed to computer manager after several incorrect password attempts, encrypt data
3. A virus is a computer program designed to damage or destroy computer programs and data in the computer. A virus can duplicate itself by passing to computer hard disks from floppy disks or across networks. Precautions: Check disks for viruses using anti-virus software, don't use outside disks on the computer
4. System crash causing damage to the data on the disk, equipment stolen and data needs reinstalling on new equipment, important files deleted accidentally and need to be recovered, hackers change data
5. c – by a company for direct mail

Index